British Sociology Seen from Without and Within

British Academy Occasional Paper · 6

British Sociology
Seen from Without and Within

Edited by

A. H. Halsey & W. G. Runciman

Published for THE BRITISH ACADEMY
by OXFORD UNIVERSITY PRESS

Oxford University Press, Great Clarendon Street, Oxford OX2 6DP

Oxford New York
Auckland Bangkok Buenos Aires Cape Town Chennai
Dar es Salaam Delhi Hong Kong Istanbul Karachi Kolkata
Kuala Lumpur Madrid Melbourne Mexico City Mumbai Nairobi
São Paulo Shanghai Singapore Taipei Tokyo Toronto

Oxford is a registered trade mark of Oxford University Press
in the UK and certain other countries

Published in the United States
by Oxford University Press Inc., New York

British Library Cataloguing in Publication Data
Data available

ISBN 0–19–726342–9   978–0–19–726342–6

Typeset by
J&L Composition, Filey, North Yorkshire
Printed in Great Britain
on acid-free paper by
Antony Rowe Limited
Chippenham, Wiltshire

Contents

Contents

Notes on Contributors

Martin Bulmer is Professor of Sociology at the University of Surrey and Director of the ESRC Question Bank. He is also Editor of *Ethnic and Racial Studies*, an international journal. He is a Vice-President of the Research Committee on the History of Sociology of the International Sociological Association. His publications include *The Chicago School of Sociology* (1984) and, with K. Bales and K. K. Sklar, eds, *The Social Survey in Historical Perspective, 1880–1940* (1991).

Colin Crouch is Professor of Governance and Public Management at Warwick University Business School. He was formerly Chair of the Department of Social and Political Sciences and Professor of Comparative Social Institutions at the European University Institute, Florence. His research interests include changes in economic governance, institutions of local economic development, the economic sociology of Europe, including central and eastern Europe, and work and industrial relations. His publications include *Social Change in Western Europe* (1999) and *Capitalist Diversity and Change: Recombinant Governance and Institutional Entrepreneurs* (forthcoming 2005). He is a Fellow of the British Academy.

Robert Erikson is Professor of Sociology at the Swedish Institute for Social Research, Stockholm University. His research interests concern social stratification, education, family, and health, especially the study of individual change over the life course and how it can be understood with regard to individual and structural conditions. He is a Fellow of the Royal Swedish Academy of Sciences, the British Academy, and the Academia Europaea, and an Honorary Fellow of Nuffield College, Oxford.

John Ermisch is Professor of Economics at the Institute for Social and Economic Research and a Fellow of the British Academy.

Formerly, he was Bonar-Macfie Professor in the Department of Political Economy at the University of Glasgow (1991–4) and a Senior Research Officer at the National Institute of Economic and Social Research. From 1991 to 2001, he was Co-Editor of the *Journal of Population Economics*, and was President of the European Society for Population Economics in 1989. His research is broadly concerned with how the family and markets interact. He is the author of *The Political Economy of Demographic Change* (1983), *Lone Parenthood: An Economic Analysis* (1991), and *An Economic Analysis of the Family* (2003), as well as numerous articles in economic and demographic journals.

Roderick Floud is President of London Metropolitan University and a Fellow of the British Academy.

A. H. Halsey is Emeritus Professor of Sociology at Oxford University and Emeritus Fellow of Nuffield College. He was a student at the London School of Economics from 1947 to 1952. He has written many books of which the latest is *A History of Sociology in Britain: Science, Literature, and Society* (2004). He is a Fellow of the British Academy.

J. D. Y. Peel has been Professor of Anthropology and Sociology at the School of Oriental and African Studies since 1989. Before then he was for fourteen years Charles Booth Professor of Sociology at the University of Liverpool. His main writings are *Aladura: A Religious Movement among the Yoruba* (1968), *Herbert Spencer: The Evolution of a Sociologist* (1971), *Ijeshas and Nigerians* (1983), and *Religious Encounter and the Making of the Yoruba* (2000). He is a Fellow of the British Academy.

Jennifer Platt is Emeritus Professor of Sociology at the University of Sussex. She is currently President of the Research Committee on the History of Sociology of the International Sociological Association. Her major research interest in the history and sociology of sociology is expressed in publications listed in the bibliography of her chapter.

W. G. Runciman is a Fellow of Trinity College, Cambridge, and served as President of the British Academy from 2001 to 2005. His books include *Relative Deprivation and Social Justice* (1966), *A Treatise on Social Theory* (three volumes, 1983, 1989, 1997), and *The Social*

Animal (1998). He chaired the Royal Commission on Criminal Justice in England and Wales of 1991–3.

Dominique Schnapper is Professor at the École des Hautes Études en Sciences Sociales and a member of the Consei constitutionne. She was awarded the Balzan Prize for Sociology in 2002. Her main publications include *Jewish Identities in Contemporary France* (1983), *Community of Citizens* (1998), *La relation à l'autre* (1998), *Qu'est-ce que la citoyenenté?* (2002), and *Providential Democracy* (forthcoming 2005).

John Scott is Professor of Sociology at the University of Essex. He has previously taught at the University of Bergen, the University of Leicester, and the University of Strathclyde. His publications include *Sociology* (with James Fulcher, 2003), *The Oxford Dictionary of Sociology* (with Gordon Marshall, 2005), *Power* (2001), *Rethinking Class: Culture, Identities, and Lifestyle* (editor with R. Crompton, F. Devine, M. Savage, 2004), and *Models and Methods in Social Network Analysis* (editor with P. Carrington and S. Wasserman, 2005).

Pat Thane is Leverhulme Research Professor of Contemporary British History at the Institute of Historical Research, School of Advanced Study, University of London.

1.
Introduction

W. G. RUNCIMAN

It was a particular pleasure for me, as the first sociologist in the hundred-year history of the British Academy to be elected its President, to introduce the conference on twentieth-century British sociology organized by Professor Halsey and sponsored jointly by the Academy and the British Sociological Association which was held at the Academy on 13 and 14 May 2004.[1] Its central theme was provided by two recently published books—one by Chelly Halsey himself on the history of British sociology,[2] and one by Professor Jennifer Platt on the history of the British Sociological Association[3]—and the discussants who had been invited from other countries and other disciplines all agreed to make their contributions at the meeting available for publication in this volume.

Any reader of this Introduction who has also read the personal observations which I, alongside seven other sociologists, contributed at his request to Chelly Halsey's book will have seen that I allowed myself some slightly disobliging remarks about my own University of Cambridge and its role—or lack of one—in twentieth-century British sociology. For similar reasons, it may be appropriate if I here allow myself some slightly disobliging remarks about the British Academy. By now, the humanities and social sciences, for which the British Academy is responsible under its Royal Charter in the same way that the Royal Society is responsible for the physical and biological sciences, cover between them a wide and complex range of increasingly specialized disciplines.

---

[1] It was also a particular pleasure to be able, on behalf of the meeting, to congratulate in his presence the undisputed *doyen* of British sociology, David Lockwood, on his forthcoming award of an honorary doctorate from the University of Cambridge.

[2] A. H. Halsey, *A History of Sociology in Britain* (Oxford: Oxford University Press, 2004).

[3] Jennifer Platt, *The British Sociological Association: A Sociological History* (Durham: sociology-press, 2003).

Many of the Academy's eighteen constituent sections embrace sub-disciplines which are coming to have increasingly little in common with one another in either substance or method. But at the beginning of the twentieth century, the entire field was subdivided into four sections only: history and archaeology taken together, philology, philosophy, and jurisprudence and economics taken together. The curious union of these last two was dissolved by an amicable divorce in 1919. But it was not until 1966 that a single section for social and political studies was created; it was not until 1983 that political studies became a separate section; it was not until 1994 that a section was created in which social anthropology and human geography were combined; and only in 1999 was a psychology section established separately from what had by then become the section in which sociology remained alongside demography, criminology, and social statistics. The Academy is currently embarking on one of its periodic reviews of its organization and structure. But whether sociology will emerge from it as an autonomous discipline with a section of its own remains to be seen.

It is perhaps to be expected that any national body of this kind will be cautious about recognizing a field of study which is not yet fully established or which might be thought to fall outside its remit. But neither of these could plausibly be said to apply to sociology. Not only can the British sociological tradition be traced back to the Scottish Enlightenment and before, but Herbert Spencer himself was still alive when the British Academy was founded.[4] Nor would it be plausible to suggest that sociology was held to be compromised as an academic discipline by its association with issues of public policy. Although it is easy to point to sociologists who are overtly committed to either support for or disagreement with the principles and policies of successive governments of the day, the same is no less true of economists. Whatever the intellectual or institutional reasons for which British economics has enjoyed a degree of prestige which British sociology has lacked, why should sociology not have been accorded earlier recognition as an autonomous discipline in its own right?

Part of the answer may lie in the story which Halsey tells in the third chapter of his book about the way in which British sociology

---

[4] Spencer was naturally invited to be a founding fellow of the Academy. But he declined, just as he had some years before declined election to fellowship of the Royal Society.

has for many years been pulled in two opposite directions, by those on the one side who want to make it into a branch of science and those on the other side who want to make it into a branch of literature. Halsey aptly quotes Wolf Lepenies's characterization of 'cultural studies' as 'an abstract of English intellectual history since Matthew Arnold: they are a blend of sociology and literary criticism';[5] and although such a blend is not unique to Britain, there is perhaps something quintessentially English in the writings of those whom Halsey cites as examples—Stuart Hall, Richard Hoggart, Raymond Williams, Terry Eagleton, and Fred Inglis. At the same time, the resolute empiricism long characteristic of British science has made its influence strongly felt ever since the nineteenth- and early twentieth-century social statisticians: Halsey again has an apt quotation in Beatrice Webb's aim, as recorded in her diary in 1909, of establishing 'on a firm basis a Science of Society'.[6] There is, as Halsey says, no reason for mutually destructive antagonism between the two, and as John Scott, Colin Crouch, and Robert Erikson (who cites also John Goldthorpe) all rightly remind us, quantitative and qualitative methods are as appropriate as each other for their particular topics. No empirical sociologist will seriously deny that understanding of human behaviour can be enhanced by works of fiction (or indeed satire: Halsey's example of Michael Young's *Rise of the Meritocracy* is very much to the point). Nor, except on the wilder shores of a now fading 'postmodernism', will any literary sociologist seriously question the demonstrable results which empirical British sociology has achieved over a hundred years and more in the reportage and explanation of a wide range of observed social behaviour-patterns, whether in groups, communities, institutions, or British or any other society as a whole. But too much argument over methodology is never good for any academic discipline, and perhaps one reason why British sociology has been denied the prestige accorded to British economics or demography or psychology or anthropology is a perception that its practitioners might have devoted more of their time and energy to doing research into actual social behaviour and

[5] Wolf Lepenies, *Between Literature and Science: The Rise of Sociology* (Cambridge: Cambridge University Press, 1988), p. 195.

[6] Norman and Jeanette Mackenzie (eds), *The Diary of Beatrice Webb, I–III* (London: Virago, 1982–4), p. 175.

less to debating alternative prescriptions about how it should be done.

There is, moreover, another two-way pull to which British sociology has been, and continues to be, subjected. This is the vertical pull exerted in one direction by those who want to give sociology its autonomy by taking it up into an intellectual space of its own where the irreducibly 'social' is safely detached from psychology (let alone biology) and in the other direction by those who think that sociology can be fully established only if it is firmly grounded in psychology or biology (or preferably both). Although Durkheim was, and remains to this day, the most influential sociologist of all in the first category, Britain too had, as Halsey reminds us, its own determinedly anti-Spencerian theorist in L. T. Hobhouse; and although 'sociobiology' is an American, not British, creation, Britain had not only Lancelot Hogben in his chair of social biology at the LSE but also (not cited by Halsey) C. D. Darlington, whose arguments for the reduction of sociology to biology extended from *The Conflict of Science and Society* (published in 1948) to *The Evolution of Man and Society* (published in 1969). There can be few if any practising British sociologists who would now agree either with the radical Durkheimians that any proferred psychological or biological explanation of a social fact is bound to be false or with the radical sociobiologists that any authentic explanation of social facts must ultimately be grounded in the long-term maximization of inclusive reproductive fitness. But mutual antagonism between those who are, so to speak, happier being pulled upwards and those who are happier being pulled downwards is no more helpful than that between the partisans of scientific and of literary sociology. To those firmly in the first category, those in the second are suspected of an outdated pseudo-empirical positivism at best and a covertly racist genetic determinism at worst. To those firmly in the second category, those in the first are suspected of vapid metaphysical pretensions at best and deliberate neglect and distortion of well-tested evidence at worst. Gratuitously exaggerated though they may be, such caricatures are not likely to enhance the image of British sociology in the wider academic world.

Yet for all these disagreements and tensions, I do not for a moment believe that British sociology as a recognized academic discipline with its own corpus of published research, its own repertory of alternative methods, and its own ongoing debates between rival theoretical schools is at serious risk of being undermined by irreconcilable differences of principle or purpose. The reason is simply that in the study, on whatever theory and by whatever method, of human groups, communities, institutions, and societies as such, there has been, is, and will continue to be a tacit consensus that at least some proffered conclusions stand up better than others to attempted disconfirmation; and although we may all agree that our findings are to a significant degree provisional and our theories to a significant degree underdetermined, we are committed by our own continuing activities and practices to acknowledging a difference between those that are demonstrably inaccurate, inconsistent, tendentious, or irreconcilable with other and better-attested evidence and those which their critics find it difficult if not impossible to discredit or overturn. The distinction is implicitly acknowledged even by those teachers of sociology who are most anxious to enthuse their students with the subversive rhetoric of philosophers like Richard Rorty or Paul Feyerabend. The questioning of received theories and methods is, and has always been, intrinsic to the practice of science and scholarship. But it depends for its intended effects on meeting some intersubjective criterion of validity without which it merely defeats its own purpose at the same time as the purposes of those whose pretensions it claims to have unmasked. We may all agree with Nietzsche that there is no truth independent of its context. But we have also to agree with him that there are truths which, in his characteristic way of putting it, have to be acknowledged as among what he called the 'irrefutable errors of mankind'. In the actual conduct of serious professional research, quotations from Rorty or Feyerabend have no more practical relevance to, say, John Goldthorpe and his colleagues on the Oxford Social Mobility study than Zeno's paradox to a team of experts in ballistics.

This is not to deny—nor has any sociologist I can think of ever done so—that the study of collective human behaviour raises controversial issues relevant to the conduct of public policy of a kind which research in the natural sciences does not. Halsey quotes Raymond Aron's rather unkind characterization of British sociology in the aftermath of the Second World War as 'essentially an attempt to make intellectual sense of the political problems of the Labour

Party',[7] and it is of course true that much of the writing of Richard Titmuss or Peter Townsend or Michael Young, like the Fabians before them, has been directly concerned with what governments, whether Labour or otherwise, ought to be doing to improve the condition of the British people. But the policy prescriptions with which their readers are free to disagree if they choose can be debated separately from those of their findings which readers of all political persuasions have no choice but to accept. Those, for example, who reject outright Townsend's definition of poverty as, according to his critics, a wilful conflation of the notion of deprivation with that of inequality are still the beneficiaries of the extensive and detailed information on the conditions of the relatively disadvantaged set out in his *Poverty in the United Kingdom* of 1979. Again, the parallel with the writings of Britain's leading economists is obvious: readers of the work of James Meade or Amartya Sen (or, for that matter, Keynes himself) are free to accept their conclusions about postulated causes and observed effects without being bound to agree with them about how governments ought to translate these conclusions into action in the hope of creating, by their chosen standards, a better world.

What has, on the other hand, always been missing in Britain is the tradition long familiar in Germany of the university professor, as Goethe's biographer Nicholas Boyle puts it, as 'secular preacher, or preceptor of the nation'.[8] Halsey would like to see sociologists have more impact than they do on how society responds to their writings, and shares with Anthony Giddens the hope that they may again become 'public intellectuals' of the kind, presumably, that Hobhouse or Beatrice Webb once were. But do sociologists who take the role of secular preacher upon themselves advance the influence and prestige of sociology by doing so? Why should professors of sociology be supposed to be any wiser or more authoritative than other people in their personal visions of the good society and their personal wishes about how they might be realized? Wasn't Max Weber right to say that sociology can tell people what they *can* do, sometimes what they *want* to do, but never what they *ought* to do? The outstanding current exemplar of the German tradition of secular preaching is Jürgen Habermas, who is some-

---

[7] *History of Sociology in Britain*, p. 70.

[8] Nicholas Boyle, *Goethe: The Poet and the Age, I* (Oxford: Clarendon Press, 1991), p. 18.

times referred to by those who cite his writings as a sociologist. But that is rather like citing Hegel as a historian rather than as a philosopher of history.[9] Habermas's version of the 'critical theory' of the Frankfurt school is grounded in a close familiarity with significant periods and topics in modern European history. But his vision of a world of rational communication free of false consciousness and abuse of power neither entails nor is entailed by his reading of the story of the emergence and significance of *Öffentlichkeit*—the bourgeois public sphere. For British sociologists, the example of Hobhouse is not encouraging, and in the case of the Webbs, Halsey again has the apt, if as he says 'wickedly satirical', quotation—Malcolm Muggeridge's account of the interment in Westminster Abbey of 'two distinguished upholders of Soviet Dictatorship'.[10] This is not to imply that British sociologists are not entitled to voice whatever may be their political views, and still less that they should pretend that they have none. But the more strenuous their attempts to use their sociology to promote their personal credos the more they risk doing their reputations as sociologists more harm than good.

A different concern, voiced by John Urry as quoted by John Scott (below, p. 140), is that the advances made by the more specialized social sciences and their accompanying encroachment into areas which sociologists have been disposed to regard as their own will lead to a progressive fragmentation of sociology to the point that it is relegated to merely 'residual' status, or becomes what Colin Crouch (below, p. 133), quoting John Westergaard, calls a 'diaspora subject'. Unwise though it is ever to predict the future of any academic discipline, I have again to say that I regard this concern as unfounded. Sociology will remain, as it has always been, the general study of collective, institutionalized human behaviour across differences of culture and history, just as psychology will

---

[9] Symptomatic of this confusion over terminology is the volume edited by Quentin Skinner which was published under the title *The Return of Grand Theory in the Human Sciences* by the Cambridge University Press in 1983. The theorists discussed, in addition to Habermas (by Giddens), are Gadamer, Derrida, Foucault, Kuhn, Rawls, Althusser, and Lévi-Strauss. With the exception of the last, the idea that these are practitioners of the 'human sciences' can only strike economists, linguists, demographers, psephologists, psychologists, archaeologists, criminologists, and human geographers—not to mention empirical sociologists—as eccentric if not downright absurd.

[10] *History of Sociology in Britain*, p. 19.

remain the general study of the workings of the minds of individual people in all the diverse environments in which they are reared and by which they are influenced, and biology will remain the general study of living organisms in all their astonishingly complex particularity. If advances in psychology and biology help to further our understanding of collective human behaviour-patterns, so much the better for sociology; and if the specialized social sciences such as economics, demography, geography, and the rest can do likewise, then once again so much the better. I am therefore in entire agreement—with one significant reservation—with John Scott when he says (below, p. 141) that the unifying centre of the discipline remains the 'study of society'. The reservation is simply that that must not be construed to mean either ruminations about the human condition in abstraction from actual social behaviour as observed at specific places and times or exclusive focus on 'societies' as precisely delineated autonomous systems. Scott's general point, however, is surely valid, as is Crouch's (below, p. 135), about the centrality of the concept of an 'institution' within the sociological tradition. The dictum that the fundamental problem of sociology is the 'problem of order' may not be uttered quite as frequently or as categorically as it used to be. But it rightly emphasizes the familiar but perennially remarkable fact that human beings down the ages and across the globe have somehow evolved a capacity for initiating and sustaining an extraordinary variety of distinctive social behaviour-patterns which cohere to the point that they can be classified and analysed as such.

This, obviously, is not the appropriate place for me to start arguing for my own recent writings in neo-evolutionary theory. But when Halsey, having said (below, p. 16) that he has been 'impressed' by the claim which I have made for the application of the Neo-Darwinian (as opposed—emphatically—to the Social-Darwinian) paradigm to sociology, then goes on to say that he is reminded of the disputes about evolutionary theory within the British sociological establishment in the first decade of the twentieth century, I feel bound to reply that the terms of the debate have since then been fundamentally and irreversibly changed. Whatever it should be replaced by, teleology is now dead, whether in Hobhouse's Whiggish version of cumulative moral progress or in Marx's version of an inevitable dialectic leading from feudalism through capitalism to communism (or, for that matter, in the Neo-Spencerian version of cumulative 'modernization', or in Weber's version of inexorable technical rationalization and spiritual disenchantment). However far—and it is a very long way—sociologists still have to go before they understand exactly how distinctive human communities, institutions, and societies come to be as they are and function as they do, the agenda is no longer dictated by a presupposition that sociology, whether scientific or literary, ought somehow to be capable of predicting what the destiny of mankind is going to turn out to be.

So although I understand the reasons for Halsey's pessimism (below, p. 21) about the future of sociology, I do not share it. Of course there will still be some of Max Steuer's 'pretend social science',[11] just as there will be some sterile disputes, some disappointing dead-ends, some inherently flawed attempts at theory-building, some vacuous elaborations of taxonomies, and some would-be innovative research programmes which fail to live up to their promise. But I am confident that in another hundred years' time sociologists world-wide will have a much better understanding than we do of just what are the possibilities, constraints, repertories, and mechanisms which account for human collective behaviour-patterns, just as I am confident that psychologists will have a better understanding of the workings of the individual minds of the men and women whose collective behaviour-patterns they are. And I am confident too that the British Academy will be there to continue to play its part in supporting British sociology alongside whatever other more or less specialized disciplines may by then be subdividing between them the scientific and scholarly study of human behaviour in all its multifarious and unpredictable forms.

---

[11] Halsey's reference is to Max Steuer, *The Scientific Study of Society* (London: Kluwer, 2003).

The View from Within

2.
The History of Sociology in Britain

A. H. HALSEY

A sober summary of the history of sociology in a short essay is impossible. Let me therefore begin at the end with the epilogue of my book.[1] I asked seven sociologists, whom I took to be representative of current strands in the subject, what they would have done if invited to write such a history, and I enclosed drafts of my first ten chapters. Their replies were mainly autobiographical and I will return to them. But it set me thinking. Why don't I tell you what they didn't say? And that led me to choose my main topic in this introductory essay: the battle between literature and science for domination of sociology. The topic fascinated me and is, I believe, rather neglected as a theme of our history if also perhaps overheated nowadays in exchanges over relativism between the denizens of 'cultural studies' and the proponents of a 'science of society'. I will therefore concentrate on the ownership of the subject. My thesis is that, as I see it, traditionally the social territory belonged to literature and philosophy. A challenge was then raised by science especially in the nineteenth century. Then, especially in the twentieth century, social science developed so as to turn a binary contrast into a triangular one.

But first let me ask the preliminary question. What are the origins of sociology?

L. T. Hobhouse offered an answer in his inaugural lecture in 1907. Sociology had three sources in Western thought: one literary—political philosophy; one quasi-scientific—the philosophy of history; and one scientific—biology. The Darwinian revolution and its Spencerian interpretation had dominated Hobhouse's youth in the 1860s and 1870s. He also recognized a fourth

---

[1] A. H. Halsey, *A History of Sociology in Britain: Science, Literature, and Society* (Oxford: Oxford University Press, 2004).

institutional source for the general 'science of society' in the philosophers of the Scottish Enlightenment led by Adam Smith in the eighteenth century and followed by John Stuart Mill in the nineteenth. If we add the names of Ferguson and Millar in Scotland, Herbert Spencer in Victorian England, and of Hobhouse's Scottish contemporaries, Patrick Geddes and R. M. McIver, as well as such social researchers as Booth and Rowntree, and the social accountancy of the statistical societies of Manchester, Bristol, and London, we can see that a great tradition of sociological theory and research has existed in Britain stretching back at least to the beginnings of the Royal Society and the 'invisible college' of the seventeenth century.

Now let me take you back to Newton's time—Britain in the seventeenth century. At that time Western Europe was economically poor, politically unevenly developed, and socially familistic and localized. Look at it now: economically rich, politically nationalized and internationalized, socially urbanized, geographically mobile, integrated into larger and larger units, able to communicate instantly and globally, less dependent on kin, linked more by secular schooling and entertainment and less by organized religion. We now live in an age of information. Gellner famously wrote: 'At the basis of the modern social order stands not the executioner but the professor.'

Where then, I wondered, is sociology to be placed in this vast transformation of economy, polity, and society?

You hardly need reminding that the history of sociology in the twentieth century has been accompanied by much noisy dispute. Malcolm Bradbury's *History Man* was a sociologist. J. L. Carr, in *The Harpole Report*, invented a large sixth-former who runs off with the headmaster's wife and is then admitted to the LSE to read, you can guess, sociology. No wonder that some, whether in the name of traditional scholarship or in defence of the morals of the young, would forbid its teaching to undergraduates.

Darwin's theory, admittedly, was initially given a powerful twist by Spencer's individualistic sociology and developed, especially in the United States of America, as social Darwinism—the survival of the fittest. The opposite consequence was also generated. Durkheim formulated an anti-Spencerian collectivism. Hobhouse too put forward an English type of anti-Spencerian theory linked closely to the doctrine of progress so predominant in his lifetime, perpetuated by the Whig version of history. But it was social Darwinism that gave rise to the academic separation and ideological hostility which subsequently arose between sociology and biology. Even today some sociologists repudiate the Darwinian legacy, asserting that sociology begins where biology leaves off, and that social Darwinism and social biology were always contaminated by racism, by Spencerian individualism, and by hereditarian prejudice.

I also noticed that, following Darwin and Galton, methodological advances were made in the use of multivariate analysis to aid pluralistic explanations. In consequence, interactionist theories replaced the older simplistic binary debates between Nature and Nurture. Genetics made spectacular strides and modern sociologists have reinterpreted the evolution of societies as a process of 'descent with modifications' free from the former preoccupation with moral progress of Hobhouse and Ginsberg.

The extension of Newtonian science from inanimate bodies to sentient human beings was the mark of the European movement of Enlightenment and the centre of the search for a science of society in which many early nineteenth-century Britons joined. Civil servants, statisticians, political arithmeticians, urban reformers, and economists were all involved.

Methods

And what, it may be added, are the methods to be used in developing a science of society? I take it that a tradition of empirical study has been handed down from its origins in the seventeenth century and the Scottish Enlightenment. Mention of either William Petty or Adam Smith is sufficient to dispose of the still widespread judgement that British sociology is a history of the mindless collection of so-called 'hard facts'. Indeed, if we look at the tradition from Adam Smith through Spencer and the Webbs, not excluding Hobhouse, and on to Giddens, Goldthorpe, and Lockwood, it is clear that social research in the UK has been addicted neither to 'abstracted empiricism' nor to 'grand theory'. The country, to be sure, has never produced a Weber or a Durkheim, but, especially since the Second World War, it has produced a solid body of theoretically sophisticated empirical studies such as the *Affluent Worker* series, *The Social Origins of Depression* (George Brown and T. Harris), or *Race, Community and Conflict* (John Rex and R. Moore). The aim has always been to seek explanations and, typically, to use them for the pragmatic improvement of human welfare.

The LSE, the Provinces, and Oxbridge

It is no accident that both sociology and social policy were placed first at the LSE, the Fabian institution invented and fostered by Sidney and Beatrice Webb in 1895. The LSE, from unlikely beginnings as a night school for part-time students, eventually evolved not only as a flourishing college of the University of London but as the principal alternative centre of social science learning in Britain, challenging the centuries-old dominance of Oxford and Cambridge.

The history of British sociology before the Second World War is in effect an aspect of the history of the LSE with its small number of Hobhousian devotees, its separate department for the training of social workers, and the underlying but powerful influence of R. H. Tawney, formally a professor of economic history, but in practice the carrier of an ethical socialist tradition which guided much of the research and teaching of 'the School' in its formative years. That outlook and reactions to it were to spread to provincial universities between 1950 and the end of the century.

But is sociology a science? Has the struggle between explanation and interpretation ceased? Only one professor in my 2001 survey confessed adherence to postmodernism. At the end of the twentieth century, W. G. Runciman declared that 'post-modernism has retreated, taking with it those aspects of the study of human social behaviour which properly belong with literature rather than science'.[2] He goes on to argue that a new evolutionary paradigm is emerging within which historical and cross-cultural hypotheses can be formulated and tested in accordance with standards shared among all the various disciplines involved in explaining why human beings are what they are and do what they do.

I was impressed but also remembered an earlier dispute from the first decade of the twentieth century when the British Sociological Society was founded. For example, the positivist Frederic

---

[2] W. G. Runciman, *The Social Animal* (London: HarperCollins, 1998).

Harrison, discussing Masterman's *The Condition of England* in the *Sociological Review* of 1909, dismissed H. G. Wells, Bernard Shaw, G. K. Chesterton, and Hilaire Belloc as 'masters of paradox and burlesque' who could 'hardly be accepted as "the sources" of scientific sociology'. The following year (1910) there appeared in the very same journal a review by S. K. Ratcliffe of 'Sociology in the English Novel' claiming that modern fiction was descriptive sociology in a larger and truer sense than the term possessed when it was used by Herbert Spencer.

So perhaps we must take seriously the thesis of Wolf Lepenies who sees the rise of sociology in the nineteenth century in Europe as located *Between Literature and Science.* In his book of that title he argues that French and German struggles for influence over the disputed territory led to an earlier formation of sociology departments in the universities of those two countries. Balzac, in *La Comédie humaine,* laid literary claims to an exhaustive description of French social structure in Comte's time, and later Zola, perhaps as impressively, in the Durkheimian climate of the Third Republic. In the British case we must ask whether Booth or Rowntree or 'the social accountants' left us with a stronger legacy, or is the depiction of industrialization, urban life, and social hierarchy best found in novels or in literary criticism or social history?

Lepenies argues that while in such countries as France and Germany sociology had developed distinct yet varying profiles as a science both opposing and supporting the Establishment, and had then within each country gone on to splinter into separate schools, in England sociology was simply a constituent of social common sense: it had no need to secure its existence by becoming an independent academic faculty.

It was not until the troubled years between the wars that we can find the origins of an academic sociology in England as well, though, to be sure, its institutionalization largely had to wait until after the Second World War. Compared with the USA, France, and Germany, Lepenies argues, 'English sociology always remained curiously pallid and lacking in distinct identity: the disciplines that came into being in England during the post-war years, and were its essential contribution to intellectual contention both at home and abroad, were so-called "cultural studies". . . . A brief characterization of what constitutes "cultural studies" would amount to an abstract of English intellectual history since Matthew Arnold: they are a blend of sociology and literary criticism.'

Notice by the way that both the arts and the sciences were once admitted to the French Academy. Buffon, the author of *Histoire naturelle*, was elected to the *Académie française* in 1753 where he spoke at his first meeting on the subject of style, and, a century later, even Baudelaire was impressed. Today the division between the Royal Society and the British Academy is rigid: only statisticians, demographers, some geographers, and some psychologists are eligible for election to both.

But what of literature and history? For an answer we must momentarily return to France where Honoré de Balzac followed Buffon with an announcement of a new and ambitious project, to extend Buffon's *Histoire naturelle* into human life. *La Comédie humaine* was justified by Balzac as 'an analogical appeal to the disciplines of history and science'. It was to be a form of social history (*histoire des moeurs*) to be understood in all its complex diversity by analogy with the taxonomic models of zoology. The animal world had been classified into *espèces zoologiques*, now the history of French society was to be portrayed as *espèces sociales*.

The novel *Eugenie Grandet* was the first venture in this huge project, to create a comprehensive drama of human life, the panorama of *espèces sociales*. Yet it seems to me to remain a descriptive but not an explanatory panorama.

The eighteenth-century Enlightenment had brought with it a wave of interest and belief in the power of Newtonian science to explain and predict the physical world. There were, at last, immutable laws governing the behaviour of bodies (including the heavenly bodies as well as the familiar tides) in an orderly universe. In the nineteenth century in Europe, this world-view was extended to the behaviour of human kind. Simple principles ruled the diversity of human activity. In Britain these principles were formulated as Bentham's utilitarianism. James Mill, a devotee of the philosophy, reared his son John Stuart in strict accordance with a puritanical version of the doctrine. John Stuart Mill's later life was a tormented struggle against paternal teaching; a passage from the culture of science to the culture of feeling, aided especially by the reading of Wordsworth and the love of Mrs Harriet Taylor whom he married in 1851. Herbert Spencer, who died in 1903, was a similar sage of the Victorian period, carrying the powerful influence of the natural sciences into the study of man. Admired by Andrew Carnegie and later by Chairman Mao in his youth, he, in John Peel's words, 'struck American universities like lightning in the early 1880s and dominated them for thirty years'.[3]

Beatrice Potter was also a Victorian child much influenced by her mentor Spencer. She too grew up believing in science, progress, and reason. In her *Diary* on 23 May 1900 she wrote: 'Our effort is now directed to one end—to establish on a firm basis a Science of Society. . . . Partly by our own individual work and partly by the [London] School of Economics. . . . We have gained university status, we have secured a building and a site, and we have the prospect of regular income, we have attracted students and we are training teachers. But how far the new activity will prove to be genuine science and not mere culture or shallow technical instruction remains to be seen.' But her later life, like J. S. Mill's, was haunted by literary ambitions. She wanted to be both the author of a new science of society and to write a novel under the title *Sixty Years On*, in which the two major themes were to be the final emancipation of women and the steady advance of state welfare services. In the event the novel remained a dream, substituted by her diaries and her two volumes of autobiography.

She married Sidney Webb in 1892. The Webbs thought of themselves as sociologists, assembling and classifying the facts of society as would zoologists with flora and fauna and then applying their results as social engineering in the guidance of social policy towards local government, trade unions, cooperatives, or poverty. These principles were observed in their book *Methods of Social Study*. While insisting on sympathetic understanding in the social sciences (and specifying Shakespeare and Goethe as exemplars of Max Weber's *verstehen*), they nonetheless stuck to their biological conception of the character of sociology.

The Claims of Literature

The novelist gripped the reading public in Victorian Britain at least as firmly as in France or Russia. Dickens began to parallel Balzac

---

[3] J. D. Y. Peel, *Herbert Spencer: The Evolution of a Sociologist* (London: Heinemann, 1971).

with a no less vast and vivid contemporaneous picture of London and of provincial life in England. And he was followed by an estimable band of novelists, including George Eliot, Thackeray, Trollope, Mrs Humphry Ward, and the Brontë sisters.

Among them Mary Ann Evans (George Eliot) may be taken as representative. We mention her here not only because, ironically, she was close to Herbert Spencer but perhaps more she was an early example of a person who espoused the cause of literature as the prime vehicle of social criticism. She was a woman, a merito-crat, of 'humble origin', a provincial nonconformist, and a moral idealist—all significant roles in the structure of Victorian society.

Men and women of letters like Balzac, Dostoevsky, Goethe, George Sand, or William Morris may be similar to sociologists and perhaps more explicitly passionate about people in society. What separates them is explanation against interpretation. The surprise is that, as social groups, they have not found ways of living together or side by side in coffee houses, salons, or university departments with less friction than they have exhibited over the past two centuries.

At all events the war went on. It divided the Webbs from H. G. Wells who in 1910 published *The New Machiavelli*, a sociological novel in which Sidney and Beatrice, thinly disguised as fictional characters, were both devotees of the uncritical faith in science pro-pounded by Herbert Spencer. Wells had joined the Sociological Society as a founding member in 1903. In 1906 he lectured to it at the LSE on 'The So-Called Science of Sociology', denying the sub-ject's scientific pretensions, demanding the destruction of Comte and Spencer as idols, and insisting that Plato was the original source of sociological thought.

After the Second World War, while cultural studies developed more or less quietly in Birmingham (under Stuart Hall's leadership from 1964), the spectacular drama was staged in Cambridge as an ill-tempered fight between C. P. Snow and F. R. Leavis. The life of F. R. Leavis, his outsidermanship at Cambridge, and his vision through *Scrutiny* of making English studies the focus of a modern university education, attracted much attention. Snow, in his Rede lecture in Cambridge in 1959, confronted and contrasted the two cultures of literature and science. In England especially, their recip-rocal hostility and prejudice—the philistinism of the scientist and the indifferent ignorance of the humanist—had dire consequences for a burgeoning scientific civilization.

The dispute, I suggest, has never ended and there we must leave it. I have tried to trace the context of the search for a science of society. The proximate impulse to the modern scientific movement lay in the human consequences of nineteenth-century industrialization. There was a challenge to both the government and voluntary civil institutions to deal with the problems of poverty, disease, and disorder that arose. Part of the intellectual response was literary—the emergence of a first culture of vigorous literature, of prose and poetry and a didactic drama of exposure in novels, pamphlets, magazines, and plays. A second culture also arose in the form of applications of Newtonian science to social affairs. Government became the focus of a scientific revolution, with heroes like Farr and heroines like Florence Nightingale devoted to developing and disseminating clear record-keeping and scientific statistics as bases of reform. Statistical societies sprang up in urbanizing Britain. Expertise rose in public life. The survey began to emerge as an instrument of social policy.

Booth and Rowntree could have been the originators of a modern British sociology. Certainly they influenced public opinion and government. But advances in the mathematical theory of probability and their application to social problems were slow to develop, especially in the universities. A network of sociology departments was particularly slow to emerge. Only after the Second World War did expansion penetrate the provincial universities to offer the possibility of a sociology firmly connected to the methodological advances made by statistics in the previous century and a half.

Let me end with a return to the epilogue of my book. Their answers are, as I said, largely autobiographical though Crouch writes most obviously in a European context. All are optimistic about the future of the subject and most are regretful about its past. I am rather pessimistic about its future, fearing especially the threat of what Max Steuer has called 'pretend social science';[4] but I am rather less condemnatory of its past. Perhaps it is as Crouch fears, a repository of the resentment of marginal groups.[5] Perhaps it will

---

[4] M. Steuer, *The Scientific Study of Society* (London: Kluwer, 2003).
[5] In Halsey, *History of Sociology in Britain*, ch. 11.

again be a source of 'public intellectuals' as Giddens hopes,[6] or even become in Runciman's phrase, 'a discipline of unchallenged scientific and scholarly standing'.[7]

Where do I stand between these authorities? Groucho Marx once stood behind a lady fumbling in her purse to pay a bill and he made an uncomplimentary remark. She turned in anger but instantly recognized that famous face. She asked, 'Would you be Groucho Marx?' 'Lady', he replied, 'what's all this about would be? I *am* Groucho Marx. Whom would you be if you were not yourself?'

---

[6] In Halsey, *History of Sociology in Britain*, ch. 11.
[7] Ibid.

3.
What Should be Done about the History of British Sociology?

JENNIFER PLATT

This essay, unlike most of the others in this collection, is as much concerned with the writing of the history of sociology as an activity as it is with the substance of what has happened in its history in Britain, although some of that substance will be drawn on for examples. My contribution was, I take it, invited because I have recently published a book (Platt 2003) not on the general history of British sociology, but on a salient part of it, the British Sociological Association (BSA). Work on the history of sociology is not usually approached through the study of its institutions, but I would argue that they deserve much more attention than they have received. In that book a fair amount of material on the general history of British sociology necessarily appears to explain the development of the BSA. But the BSA has not been merely a mirror or consequence of what was happening elsewhere; it has also been a motor of change and development which has had consequences for the history (as well as being of interest as an institution in its own right). Here some of the ways in which it has played a part in the more general history of sociology are briefly reviewed, in support of the argument for the value of more work on sociological institutions, leading into a more general discussion of lacunae in what has so far been treated and of some of the problems facing historical work in this field.

The BSA and the History of Sociology

The history of the BSA is closely entangled with the general history of higher education in Britain, and the emergence of sociology as a recognized discipline within it. If we look first at how the BSA came to be founded, in 1951, it is significant that the initial impulse came not from within academia but from meetings—involving some academics—at Political and Economic Planning (PEP),[1] a body whose general importance in the early growth of the social sciences does not seem to have been sufficiently recognized. Although the formal letters setting things in motion came from the London School of Economics, then the only real department of sociology, the first secretary of the association was from PEP. The twenty-four initial 'sponsors', drawn widely from other universities, included only three people holding posts officially in sociology (all from the LSE); most were professors of other subjects related to the social sciences. At the founding meeting, less than a third of those invited and attending were 'sociologists', though a few more shortly became such. This indicates both the low level of development of university social science at the time, and the extent to which in the universities 'sociology' still had some overtones of earlier claims to be a master, synthetic social science transcending more specialized fields. (At the same time it also remained, in the eyes of many, far from clearly distinguished from social work and social policy.)

Once founded, the BSA was for many years organizationally based at the LSE, at first formally and later less formally subsidized by it. Members of LSE staff were prominent among its committee members in the early years, and Morris Ginsberg, head of the LSE sociology department, was its first chairman and then, on his retirement, its first president. As the general dominance of LSE, with its periphery of other London institutions, was undermined by growth elsewhere, this pattern changed, and that can be traced in the changing composition of BSA committees and the growing location of its meetings outside London.

Early membership of the Association was very wide, with probably more than half the members having no connection with professional sociology or academia (Platt 2003: 22); one needs to remember that at that time there were hardly enough sociologists

---

[1] PEP was an independent organization perhaps best described now as a think-tank cum club; it brought together academics, civil servants, politicians, and businessmen, who formed working groups which produced well informed and influential reports on matters of current policy concern.

to support an association. The first conference topic was 'Social Policy and the Social Sciences', chosen for its wide appeal, with some speakers who were practitioners rather than sociologists; it was proposed to have alternate conference themes with practical rather than academic emphases in order to continue to appeal to that constituency. The presence at meetings of so many non-academics rapidly gave rise to criticism of the relevance of the discussion by those who regarded themselves as professional sociologists, and in the early 1960s a group of university sociologists began to meet separately, under the title (chosen to indicate their non-amateur status) of teachers of sociology, though not all were primarily teachers. Half their meetings were about teaching, half on research. Teaching was a hot issue at the time, as the rapid expansion of university social science meant that many departments were creating new syllabuses from scratch, and the provision of a forum for sharing ideas and information on teaching successfully met a felt need; the BSA was often consulted on such issues. Soon the organization was coopted to become a Teachers' Section of the BSA, maintaining the distinction of this subgroup from the general membership. But by 1974 sociology had become sufficiently professionalized for a separate organization to seem no longer needed, and it was closed down.

However, not all the early expansion was in what were then universities. Polytechnics[2] and colleges of advanced technology, all of which at later dates became formally universities, also contributed to it, as did teacher training colleges. Those in the polytechnics initially saw the BSA as elitist, because its university members, unlike polytechnic teachers, had research as part of their formal duties (and so were better equipped to give papers at meetings). Thus they felt distant enough from the BSA to need their own association, Sociologists in Polytechnics (SIP), which was especially active in the later 1970s; this too was eventually absorbed into the BSA. The traces of this process, which reflected the ways in which the character of the polytechnics changed despite, rather than because of, government policy in relation to them, can be seen in the changing membership of the BSA executive, with staff from (former) polytechnics emerging to prominence in the 1980s. Here

---

[2] See Jary (1979) for a valuable account of 'polytechnic sociology' as seen at the time.

too one can see the BSA playing a role in integrating different groups within the discipline.

The growth of sociology across the country was dramatic in the 1960s and early 1970s, and the shortage of sociologists with PhDs meant that many of those recruited to faculty positions were very young and, by today's standards, grossly under-qualified. This pattern probably contributed to the intellectual conflicts of the period, often connected with political stances; it was a politicized era, and this was evident in the BSA's discussions and the external issues it had to deal with, especially those connected with student unrest. Internally to the discipline, it also took important steps to deal with some of the problems which followed from the under-socialization of the intake; many junior members of faculty attended its summer schools (originated by the Teachers' Section), although these had been primarily intended for graduate students, and the first ethical code was drawn up to address some of the current issues of research practice. The system of study groups provided the opportunity for those with shared interests to meet, and some of these have played important roles in their subfields, while the annual conference brings different subfields together. The rotating locales and organizing teams of the annual conference, and the rotating editorship of *Sociology*, have given experience to many departments and allow for changing interests and viewpoints to be represented within a stable framework.

The period of the great expansion was followed by 'the cuts' in the 1980s, when numbers were reduced: few new appointments were made, and early retirements were encouraged. BSA activity then focused largely on fighting the cuts. The consequences of the trajectory of growth and decline for the demography of the discipline have been marked. Members of the earlier cohort have grown old together; significant recruitment started again only in the 1990s, and half a generation has remained missing from the smaller middle cohort. Some of the reactions to the problems caused for those seeking careers in academic sociology were played out within the BSA, which represented the discipline in such matters as pressing for the appropriate size and composition of departments to meet curricular needs, as well as putting ideological and practical resources into attempts to support members not currently employed as sociologists in maintaining their disciplinary connections.

The timing of those demographic developments meant that they had consequences for women in particular, as more came into academic life (Platt 2000). The women's movement had a considerable impact on the BSA. An organized push to improve the position of women within the Association and in sociology more widely started in 1974, and was rapidly successful in introducing new criteria of appropriate action. Formal policy on BSA activity and the language of its publications was developed to meet feminist demands; gender themes became routinely salient in conferences and study groups; it became customary for women and men to alternate in formal positions; and the Women's Caucus was given a special organizational status. In addition, codes of behaviour on gender issues were propagated more widely, and influenced action at the level of the departments. In effect there was an intersection between a formal organization and a wide social movement, providing an interesting case study of what can happen under those circumstances. (Related movements have of course taken place across the rest of higher education, and have undoubtedly contributed to significant changes in its style, practices, and personnel.) Not all those who pressed for feminist positions within the BSA were committed sociologists—some of them could be seen as engaging in entryism—and of those who were some gave priority to their feminism over sociology as such. But the movement has been so successfully institutionalized that it is now much less active, since there is little left within the BSA to protest against, and the Women's Caucus now runs activities, aimed at those new to the profession, which seem equally relevant to young men. Once again we can see how the BSA's inclusive strategy has meant that it has managed to combine space for disparate subgroups with an element of disciplinary integration. From a historical point of view it is particularly unfortunate that the deliberate strategy of the women's movement to operate informally and without conventional membership or leadership, and to keep internal documents within the closed circle of participants so that men could not see them, means that it is unusually hard to collect systematic data on it.

The women's movement has been unique in its impact, but the BSA has also been involved with other external bodies which have affected its policy and activities: it is a member of a system of interrelated organizations. Some of those, like SIP, the Teachers' Section, and Heads of Departments bodies, have been locally British and sociological; others are international and sociological (for example the International and the European Sociological Associations); others British but not specific to sociologists (for example the Economic and Social Research Council). None of these can be understood adequately without taking their relationships with the others into account, and all of them have played roles of some significance in the activities of British sociology.

The system of organizations is important everywhere, but is not the same in other countries, and comparative work on this—as on most other topics—would add to our understanding. National associations elsewhere differ in their character, in ways which also depend on local history and on the periods at which they have emerged. Thus the Canadian situation, for instance, was one where sociology had the same trajectory of expansion, but initially had a joint association with anthropology; now there is not one but two sociological associations, for the anglophone and francophone communities, institutionalizing a major social division which keeps the two sociologies apart despite their shared national identity, although the more cross-disciplinary agenda than in Britain remains.[3] In the United States, the Social Science Research Council is a federation of learned societies which has to seek its funding elsewhere (Worcester 2001), rather than a government-funded body like the ESRC, but it coexists with the governmental National Science Foundation. Some of the differences in the development of national sociologies are explained by such differences. Yet, looking at the international arena, one sees that it is not by chance that the task has come my way of writing the history of *three* social-scientific associations in the last few years, one cross-national and another both cross-national and cross-disciplinary (Platt 1998, 2002, 2003). They have all been celebrating their fiftieth anniversaries, as have similar bodies in other countries and disciplines, and these fall close to each other because the foundation of those bodies was part of, or precipitated by, the post-war settle-

---

[3] For general material on the Canadian situation, see Carroll *et al.* (1992), and for some comparative work on national associations, see the June 2002 issue of *International Sociology*.

ment of the late 1940s, in which sociology was seen as playing an important role, within the ambit of UNESCO, in promoting a peaceful future. Thus the history of sociology is connected organizationally, not only intellectually, with much larger movements of world history.

Lacunae and Desiderata

Relatively little historical work has been done in such areas. Indeed, it is surprising, given that most work in the history of sociology has been done by sociologists themselves, to note how unsociological it has been. It has tended to focus on the work of great men and—more recently—women, while the attention paid to ordinary sociologists and their routine practices, as well as to the social groups and institutions to which sociologists have belonged, has been very much less; we seem still to be anachronistically at the stage of studying the barons rather than the common people. A key methodological controversy has been between 'historicist' and 'presentist' positions—which offer alternative approaches to the issue of how to address 'the hermeneutical question of how we understand texts' (Seidman 1985: 121)—not how we understand our own social structures and their consequences. Understanding texts is an important enterprise, though often more connected with an interest in past theorists as theorists than in history as such. But even to understand texts fully it would be advantageous to know more about their socio-intellectual contexts and the circumstances under which they were produced: more data-based explanation, less freely floating interpretive 'understanding'? Moreover, however significant the work of, say, Max Weber may have become to sociologists, the process by which it has become so, and come to be treated as distinct from that of his contemporaries, is a social one not dependent only on the nature of the texts as such. It may be affected by anything from his life-span relative to that of his wife, and so whether someone was left to cultivate his reputation after his death (see Lang and Lang 1988), to the vicissitudes of (mis)translation. What the effects of the work are, in turn, will depend on decisions made about syllabuses and textbooks, on patterns of research funding, and on the nature of the publishing market, as well as on what may be the work's accidental chiming with later concerns in other societies which the writer could not have anticipated.[4]

Great (wo)men apart, what has been taken for granted by ordinary sociologists at different periods (and so perhaps left unstated explicitly) is also of considerable interest, and says more about what the general state of sociology has been at any point in time than do the distinguished works of those later canonized who were writing then. This is more likely to be manifested in textbooks and teaching documents, or in passing comments made in routine empirical research, than in innovative and original theoretical work, which is by definition atypical. These everyday background assumptions cannot be assumed to be adequately represented by the canonical texts, though they will have helped to form their writers' sense of what the issues were, and so also allow us to place those more securely in their intellectual context.

Archives and Their Limits

But, whatever the merits of those critical comments as a manifesto, our ability to act on it depends on the availability of the documents, and here there are some real problems and a need for collective action. Halsey (2004: viii) describes his own history as not 'a genuine history in the sense of systematic interpretation of primary sources'. (It may not be that, but it has the special interest which follows from looking at matters from the perspective of a well placed participant observer, and as such will also be a useful source for future historians.) If he had aimed to make it such, he would rapidly have discovered the limits of the primary sources easily available. The archives that exist are seriously inadequate, whether one is concerned with excellent central professional archives such as those at the LSE's British Library of Political and Economic Science, or the scattered papers of particular institutions or their departments. (Some of the deficiencies are described in Platt 2001.) It was striking that when I recently wrote round to a large number of university registrars to ask what seemed a very simple formal question (When was the first single-honours degree in sociology at

---

[4] Merton's use of Durkheim's 'anomie' in relation to the issue of deviance of all kinds offers a prime example of the last (Merton 1957; Cole 1975).

your university?) a high proportion wrote back referring me to the memory of the oldest member of their university's department![5] I received some very helpful replies, but what is particularly worrying about this response is that most of the oldest members of departments have retired now, and those of the earliest generation are dead; when, soon, even the youngest members of the large cohort recruited in the 1960s are no longer active, the institutional memory they carry will be gone.

Few universities appear to keep any systematic records of their own departmental histories, at either central or departmental level,[6] and the history of departments has hardly been attempted. Even such key departments as those of the LSE and Leicester have not provided departmental histories, although some fragments are available in print;[7] the first cohort of 'new' universities of the 1960s cries out for study as a group, as do the former polytechnics and the CNAA regime under which they operated. A particularly surprising gap exists in the records of teaching. It would in principle be easy to keep some records of that, since normally every course generates multiple copies of documents, with lecture titles, suggested reading, etc., which are circulated to students.[8] However, when one enquires about what can be found it often emerges that little beyond what was needed for short-term administrative purposes was ever kept, and that what records there originally were

[5] This enquiry was made as part of a project funded by the Centre for Sociology, Anthropology, and Politics (CSAP), 'Consolidating the curriculum: a pilot project to establish the feasibility of an archive of resources for the teaching of sociology'.

[6] The *Commonwealth Universities Yearbook* supplies valuable annual lists of members of university staff, by department, with their ranks and qualifications. Unfortunately, however, it has now ceased to provide complete lists, so has become a much less useful resource. Those universities which have had the old style of calendar, with staff lists and syllabus outlines as well as the dates of committees, have provided a useful source for historical work, but these have now gone out of style as a typical practice; newer universities have often only ever provided prospectuses aimed at students, which may or may not provide relatively full information on such points.

[7] Dahrendorf's (1995) history of the LSE contains some material, but its coverage is surprisingly limited if one is interested in sociology in particular. The Festschrift for Ilya Neustadt (Giddens and Mackenzie 1982) is of very limited use for this purpose. The *Sociological Review* published a useful but short series of articles on research departments, of which Scott and Mays (1960) is one example.

[8] The Teachers' Section here has played a valuable role, though not with the deliberate intention of creating historical material, because for some of its meetings collections from large numbers of departments of the documentation of courses on particular areas were circulated.

have been thrown out when the office moved, or their creator retired. (The fact that this can be explained sociologically does not, unfortunately, constitute a good excuse.) The large number of retirements taking place as the cohort of the late 1960s and early 1970s reaches retirement age exacerbates the rate of attrition. What remains is, therefore, almost certain to be an accidental sample, over-representing a few institutional and individual hero(in)es of the hoard while leaving some key areas uncovered. Perhaps we can at least do a little better than this for the future, and indeed some initiatives in that direction have been made, though their success remains to be seen. Fortunately the same problems do not apply in the case of textbooks, so it remains possible to study them, and the excellent publishers' archives at the University of Reading even provide useful background material on some of them.

Another area where insufficient work has been done is the history of empirical research, though the documentation there is better than for teaching. Some published reports of research contain useful background material as well as useful descriptions of methods; some separate accounts by researchers of their experiences and decisions are also available (for example Bell and Roberts 1984), though most of these for Britain come from the late 1970s and early 1980s heyday of such forms of reflexivity. The Mass Observation Archive at Sussex contains material on both the original Mass Observation work (which has been extensively written about) and some other research enterprises, such as the earliest days of the War-Time Social Survey (on the latter, see Platt 1986). In addition, there are at least two current undertakings which in different ways involve the retrieval and/or reuse of material on past projects; work by Goodwin and O'Connor (2003) on the Young Worker project directed by Norbert Elias, and Mike Savage's use of the original field notes from a number of famous qualitative studies as sources for the history of post-war popular identities (Savage 2005). The resources of data archives have been inadequately exploited for the history of social research, though their holdings are not usually documented for that purpose; however, Qualidata has been doing sterling work in retrieving material on at least some classic projects, and adding to their documentation, as well as archiving contemporary work (Corti and Thompson 2003). Intellectual groupings such as study groups have been very poorly documented, though at least the BSA's Medical Sociology study group has written a little about its own history (Pope and Ziebland 1993). The National Deviancy Conference had an important impact on sociology/criminology, and one well worth documenting as part of our history, and it is gratifying to be able to note that participants have indeed made some steps towards writing its history (Rock 1998; Walton and Young 1998). If members of other intellectual networks, whether more or less formal, were to document their history in the same way, that would make a valuable addition to our knowledge.

Journals obviously play a key role in the social system of sociology, and they too have been very little researched except in citation studies and similar work on their published contents. Andrew Abbott (1999) has shown how much mileage one can get from study of the workings of a journal, in his case the *American Journal of Sociology*. It is unlikely that most journals have left such rich records, but something could surely be made of the written archive that there is in minutes of editorial boards, formal reports sent up their hierarchies, editors' correspondence with publishers, etc., as well as of the memories of their editors, administrators, publishers, and contributors.

Conclusion

We would know more about the history of sociology if our work on it ranged more widely across potential topics and sources. A special case has been made here for social institutions, but one could, for instance, add to those the patterns of individual careers and how they add up to the experience of cohorts.[9] That is an argument addressed to those who work on the history of sociology, but one does not need to have a central intellectual interest in that to make a useful contribution to the archives which they need to draw on. The documentation routinely archived at present is so limited that anyone who, for instance, saves some of their main teaching

---

[9] Feminism has led considerable numbers of women to write about their career experiences (for example David and Woodward 1998), usually focusing on the obstacles in their way, but similar accounts by men, or by women for whom obstacles have been less salient, are largely absent.

materials and deposits them in a library, annotates their curriculum vitae to make a sort of professional autobiography, or collects memories and records of the early days of their department, is providing potentially valuable material for the future historian. Why not do it?

References

Abbott, Andrew (1999), *Department and Discipline*, Chicago: University of Chicago Press.

Bell, Colin and Roberts, Helen (eds) (1984), *Social Researching*, London: Routledge & Kegan Paul.

Carroll, W. K., Christiansen-Ruffman, Linda, Currie, R. and Harrison, D. (eds) (1992), *Fragile Truths: Twenty-Five Years of Sociology and Anthropology in Canada*, Ottawa, ON: Carleton University Press.

Cole, Stephen (1975), 'The Growth of Scientific Knowledge: Theories of Deviance as a Case Study', in Lewis A. Coser (ed.), *The Idea of Social Structure*, New York: Harcourt Brace Jovanovich, pp. 175–220.

Corti, Louise and Thompson, Paul (2003), 'Secondary Analysis of Archived Data', in C. Seale *et al.* (eds), *Qualitative Research Practice*, London: Sage, pp. 327–43.

Dahrendorf, Ralf (1995), *L.S.E.: A History of the London School of Economics and Political Science, 1895–1995*, Oxford: Oxford University Press.

David, Miriam and Woodward, Diana (eds) (1998), *Negotiating the Glass Ceiling*, London: Falmer Press.

Giddens, Anthony and Mackenzie, Gavin (eds) (1982), *Social Class and the Division of Labour*, Cambridge: Cambridge University Press.

Goodwin, John and O'Connor, Henrietta (2003), 'The Young Worker Project Renewed', in E. Dunning and S. Mennell (eds), *Norbert Elias*, London: Sage.

Halsey, A. H. (2004), *A History of Sociology in Britain*, Oxford: Oxford University Press.

Jary, David (1979), *The Development of Sociology in the Polytechnics*, SIP Paper 6, mimeo.

Lang, Gladys Engel and Lang, Kurt (1988), 'Recognition and Renown: The Survival of Artistic Reputation', *American Journal of Sociology* 94, pp. 79–109.

Merton, Robert K. (1957), 'Social Structure and Anomie', in Merton, *Social Theory and Social Structure*, Glencoe, IL: Free Press, pp. 131–60.

Platt, Jennifer (1986), 'Qualitative Research for the State', *Quarterly Journal of Social Affairs* 2, pp. 87–108.

Platt, Jennifer (1998), *A Brief History of the ISA: 1948–1997*, Madrid: International Sociological Association.

Platt, Jennifer (2000), 'Women in the British Sociological Labour Market 1960–1995', *Sociological Research Online* 4, 4, 16 pp, www.socresonline.org.uk/4/4/platt, html.

Platt, Jennifer (2001), 'National Needs for the Sociological Archive—and the British Situation', in Janusz Mucha, Dirk Kaesler, and Wlodimierz Winclawski (eds), *Mirrors and Windows*, Torun: Nicholas Copernicus University Press, pp. 311–25.

Platt, Jennifer (2002), *Fifty Years of the International Social Science Council*, Paris: International Social Science Council.

Platt, Jennifer (2003), *The British Sociological Association: A Sociological History*, Durham: sociologypress.

Pope, C. and Ziebland, S. (1993), 'The BSA Medical Sociology Group: 25 Years On', *Medical Sociology News* 19, 1, pp. 12–16.

Rock, Paul (ed.) (1988), *A History of British Criminology*, Oxford: Clarendon Press.

Savage, Mike (2005), 'Working-Class Identities in the 1960s: Revisiting the Affluent Worker Study', *Sociology* 39, 5.

Scott, W. H. and Mays, J. B. (1960), 'Department of Social Science, University of Liverpool', *Sociological Review* 8, pp. 109–17.

Seidman, Steven (1985), 'Classics and Contemporaries: The History and Systematics of Sociology Revisited', *History of Sociology* 6, pp. 121–35.

Walton, Paul and Young, Jock (eds) (1998), *The New Criminology Revisited*, Basingstoke: Macmillan.

Worcester, Kenton W. (2001), *The Social Science Research Council, 1923–1998*, New York: SSRC.

4.
Sociology in Britain in the Twentieth Century: Differentiation and Establishment

MARTIN BULMER

The two works by Chelly Halsey and Jennifer Platt (Halsey 2004; Platt 2003) which form the theme for this volume raise some very stimulating questions about the development of British sociology in the twentieth century, but they do not exhaust those questions. Taken together with the eight contributions to Chelly Halsey's epilogue (pp. 203–24), two written by Halsey and Platt and six by leading contemporaries—Zygmunt Bauman, Colin Crouch, Anthony Giddens, Ann Oakley, W. G. Runciman, and John Westergaard—they throw out a number of important questions. My purpose here is to raise what seem to be significant questions stimulated by the two books, by the eight commentaries, and by the two-day conference held at the British Academy in May 2004.

Who Should Write the History of Sociology?

Having acquired a copy of Chelly Halsey's book in the Economists Bookshop in late April 2004, I ran into a former senior colleague of mine, considerably older than me, at an LSE conference the same day. I mentioned the book, and he expressed interest. On being shown it, he responded in characteristic fashion by looking up his name in the index, and then spending five minutes reading every entry in which Halsey had something to say about him. At the end, to my relief, he professed himself satisfied as to what he found. To write the history of one's own discipline is to face the dual problem that one is part of the history that one writes about, and one runs the risk that one's coevals may turn round and refute propositions that one is advancing. This has not, of course, inhibited members of the history profession from commenting in trenchant terms upon the activities of their contemporaries (for example Marwick 1970; Kenyon 1983) but historians are rightly sceptical about oral, retrospective testimony as against the historical record in documents. Such issues raise the question: is the history of sociology a task for the self-reflective sociologist or for the professional historian?

In the conference, the key works are written by sociologists, Chelly Halsey and Jennifer Platt. A note of caution is in order. How well judged is their focus ? How well placed are our two authors, as contemporary participants, to act as historians of events of which they themselves have been a part? Halsey, for example, as a member over time of sociology groups at the LSE (as a student), Liverpool, Birmingham, and Oxford, Platt as sometime President of the British Sociological Association, of which she now writes the history, were both participants in the events about which they write. Halsey's history is based on extensive personal knowledge and experience in the sociological world from the centre, and is handled in a masterly fashion. Nevertheless, it is written from a particular perspective, that of the 'Golden Triangle' of London and Oxbridge, perhaps at the expense of similar developments elsewhere, which is surprising given the author's experiences in Liverpool and Birmingham. The perspective of the book is that of the dominant early department at the LSE. Though they are mentioned, there are few details about the Leicester department headed by Neustadt, Manchester under Gluckman and Worsley, Liverpool under Simey, or Edinburgh under Tom Burns. Jennifer Platt perhaps sidesteps the problem more adeptly, because her history of the BSA is solidly grounded in documents which provide the record of the Association's activities. Sometimes these seem a bit dry, but they have been complemented by interviews with participants, though this again brings one up against the fallibility of retrospective recollection. One of the problems of disciplinary institutional history such as this is what standpoint to adopt and where to place the focus.

The alternative is to get historians to write the history. Sometimes—the late Philip Abrams is a good example—the author may be in transition from history to sociology, and *The*

Origins of British Sociology, 1832–1914 (Abrams 1968) was an interpretative essay by a neophyte sociology lecturer well trained in
British history. Other studies of the history of the social sciences in
the UK have been written by professional historians such as José
Harris (1977) and Reba Soffer (1977). In the USA, work on the history of the social sciences and their underpinnings by Donald
Fleming (1967), Barry Karl (1974, 1987), and Robert C. Bannister
(1987, 2003) provide examples of the fruitfulness of studies by professional historians. For a broader view, see Porter and Ross (2003).

Who Counts as a Sociologist?

Sociology may be considered as an intellectual activity, an established academic discipline, or an institutionalized form of knowledge, which one recognizes with reference to the figures in the
Pantheon of that particular discipline or field. As Philip Abrams
pointed out nearly forty years ago, British sociology has a long
history among people who did not call themselves sociologists and
did not contribute to the institutionalized activity as we know it
today. Some came to the field as social investigators, and the
history of British social investigation is a distinguished one,
overlapping, but not quite the same as, the history of British
sociology.

Chelly Halsey rightly dwells upon the tradition of political
arithmetic, though perhaps he takes it back too far. The nineteenth-
century sources of British sociology in social investigation are
surely the most important—the blue books, the investigations of
public health, Henry Mayhew, the National Association for the
Promotion of Social Science, Charles Booth, Seebohm Rowntree,
and as we turn into the twentieth century A. L. Bowley. Many of
these figures, however, are also seen as part of the tradition of
British social policy, while some British sociologists would not
recognize them as their ancestors.

Among academics and thinkers, there are many with distinguished claims to have contributed to the development of social
thought whom one would nevertheless hesitate to call sociologists.
To illustrate the point, I cite a few names from the latter part of the
nineteenth century, including T. H. Green, Sir Henry Maine, F. W.
Maitland, Herbert Spencer, Sidney and Beatrice Webb. All made

sociological contributions without being sociologists. When one moves into the twentieth, the list could be made longer, but it is more apt in this context to focus upon the two books under consideration.

Jennifer Platt records that at the meeting in October 1950 at which the British Sociological Association was established, only one-third of the seventy people attending could be regarded as 'sociologists', the remainder coming from other social science and humanities disciplines. Of the twenty-seven signatories of the initial public letter calling for the establishment of the BSA, headed by the director of the LSE, Alexander Carr-Saunders (a demographer by origin), at most six held posts in sociology (Ginsberg, Glass, T. H. Marshall, Simey, Sprott, and Wootton), and the remainder, apart from the Director of Political and Economic Planning, academic posts in other social sciences or philosophy. They included Frederic Bartlett, Cyril Burt, C. A. Mace, and T. H. Pear in psychology, G. D. H. Cole in political theory, Gordon Childe in archaeology, H. J. Habbakuk in economic history, Sargant Florence, Percy Ford, and Brinley Thomas in economics, Raymond Firth and Meyer Fortes in social anthropology, and Richard Titmuss in social policy.

The issue of who can be regarded as a sociologist is not settled by devices like the setting up of the Sociology Teachers' Section which took place within the BSA in 1964. This provided a home for a while for those who regarded themselves as professional sociologists, distinguishing them from the more general early membership of the BSA. Many such members were on the fringes of the nascent discipline, whose claim to be called 'sociologist' was fairly weak. But who is to count as a 'sociologist'? In the mid- and later twentieth century, to take them in alphabetical order, how would one classify Mark Abrams, Mark Benney (1966), Henry Durant, Tom Harrisson, the founder of Mass Observation (Heimann 1998), Richard Hoggart, Charles Madge, Bronislaw Malinowski (Young 2004), Leon Radzinowicz (1999), R. H. Tawney (Terrill 1973), or Peter Willmott (1985)? None of them apart from Benney (in the USA) and Madge held chairs in sociology, and even they were hardly typical; Benney was by origin a burglar, self-educated in prison (1936), and Madge a poet who had participated in Mass Observation. Like Herbert Spencer and Max Weber in an earlier period, much sociology was carried out by people whose primary identification for much of their life was not as a sociologist.

As part of his research, Chelly Halsey conducted a systematic postal social survey of all professors of sociology in the United Kingdom in 2001, drawn from the *Commonwealth Universities Yearbook* supplemented by his own reading and memory. Information about deceased professors is included, drawn from other sources described as 'public and private records', so the list (pp. 225–32) is a reasonably comprehensive list of British sociologists to have reached professorial rank by 2001. Here again, however, demarcation becomes an issue.

While scanning a list of people a few of whom one has never heard of, mirth is occasioned by the following footnote which appears against four names, one each on pp. 227, 228, 230, and 232: 'Not formally a professor: included in error.'

The names are:

- Norbert Elias, who retired in the UK as a reader at Leicester University, but achieved great fame after retirement;
- Ruth Glass, wife of David, who was Director of the Centre for Urban Studies at UCL;
- W. G. Runciman, who is Senior Research Fellow of Trinity College, Cambridge;
- Lord Young of Dartington (Michael Young), who at his death was Director of the Institute of Community Studies.

Yet all are distinguished sociologists whom it would be absurd to exclude from a list of major twentieth-century British sociologists. The problem of demarcation remains a difficult one.

Is One Optimistic or Pessimistic about the Future of Sociology?

Sociology in Britain, particularly if one defines 'sociologist' broadly, as in the preceding section, has many distinguished nineteenth-century precursors. The early years of the twentieth century saw the establishment of the first chair in the subject, at the LSE. Yet by comparison with the nineteenth century, all was not well around 1900, and the advancement of the subject was very uneven between 1850 and 1950:

> In its formative years before 1914, British sociology was exhausted by superficial repetitions and rending debates about form which ignored the more fundamental issue of contents. That premature exhaustion, from which

> British sociology recovered only after the Second World War, led to a failure
> to produce either compelling theoretical analysis or methodical practical
> programmes. (Soffer 1982: 800–1)

Edward Shils characterized British sociology during the first half of
the twentieth century in similar terms:

> In France and Germany, powerful and learned minds thought about the
> nature of society and tried to envisage modern society within the species of
> all the societies known to history. In America, sociologists busied themselves
> in villages and in city streets, carrying on the work of Booth, finding illustra-
> tions of the ideas of Simmel, Tönnies, and Durkheim and developing under
> the guidance of Robert Park a few of their own. In Britain, however, while
> social anthropology and economics flourished as in no other country, sociol-
> ogy gathered the soft dust of libraries and bathed in the dim light of ancestral
> idolatry. Here and there during these sociologically sterile decades, there was
> a momentary pulse of life but it never spread and the air of death soon
> reasserted itself. Graham Wallas on politics, Tawney on the culture of class,
> Hogben, Ginsberg and Laski on social selection, Marshall in one excellent
> and forgotten essay on the British aristocracy, gave off some sparks which no
> one even nurtured into a small flame. Karl Mannheim quickened the pulse of
> British undergraduate and foreign students for a time but he found little
> intellectual hospitality among his coevals. (Shils 1985: 166)

Halsey and Platt take the story forward from 1950, and show
how the academic discipline of sociology became established in the
United Kingdom during the second half of the twentieth century.
The story has been told before, but both manage to provide fresh
material and new insights into the development of the discipline,
both focusing upon its institutional forms. That sociology is now
solidly established within British academia, in the ancient universities and the British Academy as well as in newer institutions, is a
source of satisfaction to sociologists, and part of the celebratory
aspect of the history of the discipline.

And yet, writing in 2004 for Halsey's epilogue, W. G. Runciman,
a key figure in British sociology in the second half of the twentieth
century, albeit from a slightly distant position (1989), reported a
sense he had that all was not well 'institutionally speaking':

> As a collective national enterprise, British sociology did not achieve the
> recognition and influence that I would (if asked) have predicted when I
> returned to my Cambridge college in 1960 at the conclusion of a Harkness
> Fellowship held at Harvard, Columbia and the University of California at
> Berkeley. (Halsey 2004: 219)

The British Academy celebrated its centenary with a series of Centenary Histories of different disciplines, including history and political science, but there is no volume for sociology. The volume edited by Hayward, Barry, and Brown on *The British Study of Politics in the Twentieth Century* (1999) surprisingly throws quite an amount of light on the development of sociology, not only in the field of political sociology, but in other areas such as comparative government and the study of political organizations. The ghosts of Roberto Michels, Vilfredo Pareto, and Karl Wittfogel lurk among a group of scholars recognized by members of a discipline who are sometimes not notably hospitable to sociological perspectives (cf. Runciman 1963). The realm of social and political theory integrates the two fields most successfully, but political theory is perhaps a minority pursuit among political scientists. It is notable that there was not a speaker providing the viewpoint of political science in the present symposium.

Having cleared the ground, I want to turn to five issues raised by the two works by Halsey and Platt which deserve further consideration. Even if there are reasons for disappointment about the history of twentieth-century British sociology, there are nevertheless concrete achievements to celebrate, much distinguished individual scholarship to admire, and a number of salient issues to pursue.

The Political Embeddedness of Sociology

Philip Abrams argued in 1968 that sociology failed to develop in the late nineteenth and early twentieth centuries because of the range of opportunities which were available in Britain to move out of the scholarly world into the world of political action. The boundary between sociology and politics was not clean-cut but permeable. L. T. Hobhouse, first professor of sociology in the country, at the LSE, was a good example (Collini 1979). He had strong philosophical interests; politically he was a liberal and for a time he was a political reporter for the *Manchester Guardian*. The social investigator Seebohm Rowntree, pioneer student of poverty, became closely involved in the question of land reform and in advising the Liberal Party on a number of issues (Briggs 1961). Starting with T. H. Marshall, there are a number of leading sociologists who have been Labour parliamentary candidates at one time or another, though not as many as in the field of social policy. Others, such as Michael Young and Chelly Halsey himself, became for a time official or unofficial special advisers to particular government ministers. The lure or embrace of politics is not insignificant in understanding the history of British sociology and social investigation.

Around 1970, Halsey reports that the French sociologist and commentator Raymond Aron was visiting Oxford, and in the course of conversation observed: 'The trouble is that British sociology is essentially an attempt to make intellectual sense of the political problems of the Labour Party' (Halsey 2004: 70). This is the history of sociology reduced to anecdote, but a very telling one. It is of course over-simple to characterize the Nuffield College work on equality of opportunity, social stratification, and social mobility as concerned primarily with the political agenda of the Labour Party, but there was a congruence, and the work of Halsey, Floud, and later J. W. B. Douglas on equality of educational opportunity certainly did feed into the debates about comprehensive education in the late 1950s and early 1960s. The Oxford Mobility project, though severely academic in conception and execution, did provide evidence about the openness or fixity of movement between social strata which had political implications.

In the second half of the twentieth century, how far was sociology driven forward by people whose original interests were in some sense political? Halsey goes into the social origins of the influential post-war cohort of LSE sociologists, but not in any detail into their orientation to politics. Systematic evidence on this point is lacking, but many sociologists have come from political families, using that term in a broad sense. (Such connections are even stronger in a field like social policy.) British sociology has lacked a prophet like Richard Titmuss—there is a good discussion of him by Halsey on pages 196–8, emphasizing his commitment to social equality, social justice, citizenship, and welfare—but there is a sense that British sociology has been engaged in a continuing argument with politics or about issues which are central to the political agenda.

The close affinity between history and political thought as academic disciplines in Britain also has a bearing on the development of sociology. The entrepreneurial director of the Laura Spelman Rockefeller Memorial in New York, Beardsley Ruml, in 1924 offered the University of Cambridge endowment for two chairs, one in political science and one in sociology. The first was accepted and the second declined, and the political theorist Ernest Barker was appointed to the professorship of political science (Bulmer 1981). How British sociology might have developed had this offer of a chair in sociology been accepted is an interesting counterfactual. A generation later, political thought was significant in nurturing the nascent social sciences at Cambridge, as evident in the list of dedicatees in Peter Laslett's edition of John Locke's *Two Treatises on Government* in 1960. If one can decipher the initials, these students of political thought include a remarkable number who later rose to distinction in British social science.

Halsey comments on this issue on the basis of his survey results, which he suggests indicate that the sociology profession tends to have become politicized. More sociologists are on the left, and even the far left, than among academics in general. One may, he comments, 'sincerely regret that recruits to the profession are not more evenly spread across the political spectrum' (2004: 163), notwithstanding some outspoken supporters of the right among sociology professors. Of course, there is an interaction between the public reputation of sociology and those whom it recruits. If the discipline is seen as engaged in demystification and challenging the status quo, it may not recruit from among those whose families take a different view. In any case, the relationship between sociology and politics is a complex one.

Was the Dominance of the Golden Triangle inhibiting?

How far does class enter in another way into the make-up of the discipline? Is sociology located more on what Shils called the periphery rather than the centre of British society? Where sociology became established rightly gets a lot of attention in Chelly's book. The importance of the Golden Triangle is clear, and the failure of sociology to become solidly established there, particularly in Oxbridge, gets much attention. Both Halsey and Runciman express reservations about sociology at the LSE despite its centrality to the story. Why did it not achieve the élan of history at Cambridge or politics at Oxford? In the early days, it was small, and for a time Ginsberg was a curious academic leader. Marshall was more inspiring, but eventually withdrew to UNESCO. Karl Mannheim was a distinguished refugee, but felt that he was not appreciated, and took refuge in the Institute of Education. In the post-1960 period, the LSE department was considerably larger, but by then was facing competition from the newly expanding provincial universities.

Another part of the story, which gets a reasonably comprehensive treatment from Halsey, concerns the hostility to sociology at both Oxford and Cambridge:

> Why were Oxford and Cambridge so resistant? To some extent they were right in their assertion that sociology is no science, that its works are usually painfully inelegant if not outrightly barbarous in presentation and that they were often vehicles for political propaganda. But that is not anywhere near the whole story, nor at all close to the root of the matter. The central fact is that the higher type of British intellectual—the Oxford and Cambridge don or graduate of the first half of this [the twentieth] century—was usually a man of acute intelligence and fastidious standards exercised within the constraints of a narrow imagination and undeveloped heart. Sociology is a study which has for its ultimate object the ramification of the logic of heart. The narrow imagination and the undeveloped heart cannot cope with the logic of the heart as it beats in daily life and in times of crisis. (Shils 1985: 168)

The hostility to abstraction and general theory seemed to be reserved for sociology. Economists could theorize to their heart's content. Talcott Parsons made the mistake of lecturing the Cambridge economists about the theoretical framework which they should adopt, and allegedly put the cause of sociology back ten years. On the part of some Cambridge historians, on the other hand, notwithstanding the optimism and relative openness of Trevelyan (1913), E. H. Carr (1961), or Plumb (1969), there was evident a deep-seated loathing of conceptualization. Geoffrey Elton was an influential figure denouncing the generalizing aspirations of the social sciences (1967). Charles Wilson in his inaugural lecture lamented the use of general concepts such as 'class' or 'elite' (1964). Maurice Cowling in *The Nature and Limits of Political Science* (1963) argued that all the social sciences, when scrutinized critically, could be reduced either to history or to philosophy, and that, if they did not reduce in this way, they had not been looked at critically enough. The institutional and intellectual centrality of history in Britain (itself studied by Soffer 1994) was perhaps feeling itself under challenge.

British antipathy to sociology deserves further study. Undoubtedly it has something to do with social class and the class composition of institutions of higher learning. It has often been observed that the social background of UK academics in social anthropology differs from that in sociology, though this generalization is impressionistic rather than precise. Chelly Halsey charts the modest social origins of many of the post-war generation of LSE sociologists. Norman Birnbaum, a radical American who taught sociology at the LSE and was a fellow of Nuffield College before returning to the USA in the 1960s, once observed that Oxbridge provided the officer class, and the LSE the NCOs for British society. The role of outsiders needs more attention, not only in sociology. To confine oneself to those who settled permanently in the UK, Karl Mannheim, Viola Klein, Ilya Neustadt, Stanislav Andreski, Zygmunt Bauman, Clyde Mitchell, Theodor Shanin, John Rex, and Stan Cohen, have all left their mark on British sociology, and all originated outside the UK. Halsey mentions this as he goes along, but the issue does not really get a systematic treatment.

Is Sociology Characterized by Its Methods?

One of the characteristics which defines sociology as against history is its methodological self-consciousness. The history of British sociology has been usefully addressed from the point of view of the development of social investigation, while Jennifer Platt has illuminated the development of research methods in American sociology (Platt 1996). Gaps begin to open up among sociologists when contemplating this history, for some see quantification as more central than others (contrast Bauman 1990 with Goldthorpe 2000).

In theory, common interests in shared methodological approaches might lead to cross-fertilization across different disciplines. Though this happens to some extent, the obstacles seem to be considerable. In quantitative work, one might expect common ground to be shared between the quantitatively minded in sociology, political science, social policy, demography, and social statistics, and between the British Sociological Association, the Political Studies Association, the Social Policy Association, the British Society for Population Studies, and the Royal Statistical Society. In practice, such pursuit of interests in common is rare, and those with serious interests in quantitative exchange seem more likely to focus their efforts in the Royal Statistical Society. Among ethnographers, potential common ground between social anthropologists and sociologists is usually less evident than their differences, for example in assumptions made about the stance of the investigator as being from outside the culture altogether compared to being or trying to become an insider. Social anthropology and sociology have typically taken different stances on these questions. So a symposium such as this raises questions about the height of the fences which separate one discipline from another, and the potential for crossing the divide.

What is Sociology's Trajectory?

Where is sociology going? What are its aims as an academic discipline? The questions may seem unanswerable, and Halsey does not attempt to answer them, rather throwing light on the issue by looking back at its development. Platt does address the issue more directly because she is discussing the various initiatives taken within the British Sociological Association to advance the discipline, and particularly the vexed issue of professionalization. One basic fact is that sociology in the last half century has expanded enormously within UK higher education, and is now a secure part of academia in a way that it was not half a century ago when the BSA was established. One corollary of this is that the non-sociological membership of the BSA has largely fallen away, and the Sociology Teachers' Section no longer exists as an 'association within an association' as it did in the 1960s. Moreover, other professional associations have been formed or have expanded, including the Social Policy Association, the Social Research Association, the British Society for Population Studies, the British Society for Criminology, the British Educational Research Association, and the Evaluation Society, all of which have drawn members away from the BSA. (These and other learned societies are now organized into an umbrella organization, the Academy of Learned Societies for the Social Sciences, of which the BSA is one member.) In many respects, British sociology is less professionalized than its American counterpart, but in one regard British sociology is perhaps narrower and more focused, in excluding those from cognate disciplines from appointment to sociology posts. In the USA, it is not uncommon to find sociology departments that have within them social statisticians, demographers, social psychologists, social historians, criminologists, or others. With the possible exception of criminology, this is less common in the UK. For example, it is rare for social statisticians or demographers to hold positions in UK sociology departments, one or two places like Nuffield College, Oxford, apart.

This has had consequences, some of which are discussed in the works under review and some of which are not. Halsey is so wedded to the tradition of political arithmetic that he ignores the extent to which there may be scepticism about this line of work within British sociology. The survey tradition within social investigation is a strong one historically, but it has carried over much more into social policy than into sociology, with some exceptions. The ambivalence which British sociology displays towards quantification is not really addressed in either work, and the caesura between sociology on the one hand and social investigation on the other is not dealt with.

The growing gap between sociology and social policy, which sometimes still inhabit the same department but increasingly are separate from each other in UK universities, deserves fuller discussion. Despite the handsome tribute to Titmuss, Halsey is perhaps too close to social policy and too appreciative of it to address the issue of what has been lost by the separation. Bauman indeed argues that, in the later twentieth century, sociology has benefited from this distance:

> Perhaps in the end, that 'internal exile' turned to be British sociology's good luck. Neither spoiled by excessive public demands nor rushed by overblown and impossible-to-gratify public expectations, insured against the dangers awaiting the academics seduced into the corridors of power, sociology was free to select its own topics and could be guided by social and cultural criteria of relevance. This chance has been taken, and to great effect. (Bauman, in Halsey 2004: 207).

There remains the nettle of 'professionalization'. Platt provides a judicious discussion of the various efforts made in this direction by the BSA, including the rather decisive rejection in 1974 of moves to make the BSA more like the British Psychological Society with different categories of member and different routes of entry. Many members did not see sociology as akin to engineering, medicine, or law in requiring certification of fitness to practice. The issue has come back in a roundabout way through the Research Training Guidelines promulgated by the Economic and Social Research Council, which are a kind of attempt to impose professional standards in research training. Irving Louis Horowitz made a distinction many years ago between conceptions of sociology as a 'profession' and of sociology as an 'occupation'. The predominant British conception has always been that the pursuit of sociology is an 'occupation', with much more ambivalence about claims to professionalism.

What Sources Should We Use for the History of Sociology?

Finally, how does one re-create the history of a set of institutional developments? These two fine books provide some reflections on the sources in existence for writing the history of sociology. Both use secondary sources extensively. Several distinct types of primary source are used by both authors in different mixes. Chelly Halsey relies upon his own personal knowledge and the results of his 2001 survey of all British sociology professors, and on correspondence with leading figures arising out of his survey. Jennifer Platt starts from the archival record of the British Sociological Association, fortunately preserved in the British Library of Political and Economic Science, supplemented by personal interviews with surviving office holders in the Association and by personal knowledge. Neither are quite the blend which a professional historian would be likely to use, though some of these sources would certainly be used by them.

Two of these sources run counter to the traditional course of scholarship which urges detachment from the subject being investigated and scepticism about retrospective evidence. Both in the books and in the conference about them, personal knowledge loomed quite large. This is not necessarily incapacitating. The Hayward–Barry–Brown volume on political science (1999) could be said to be permeated by personal knowledge, yet provides an illuminating overview of the development of its subject during the twentieth century. Perhaps Halsey's theme of the tension in British sociology between a scientific, quantifying, and explanatory conception of the subject and a literary, interpretative, and cultural approach provides some justification for his reliance upon personal knowledge. Our subject is neither high politics nor the workings of the national economy, about both of which copious evidence abounds. The development of a marginal and initially small academic discipline must perforce rely upon some degree of inside knowledge, even at times anecdotal. (For an example of one such anecdote, see Runciman's remark: 'Did he [Morris Ginsberg] really say of *Wirtschaft und Gesellschaft*, as Edward Shils once told me, "I've read all that stuff and there's nothing in it."?' (Halsey 2004: 219))

Reliance upon personal interviews also lays itself open to the criticism of subjectivity. Oral history methods have often been criticized as unreliable sources of evidence. The memories of politicians are not necessarily a good source of data. As A. J. P. Taylor observed about Attlee's memoirs as told to Francis Williams, *A Prime Minister Remembers* (1965), they showed how much it was possible to forget. The benefit of hindsight can be a powerful distorting factor both in relation to individual actions and their interpretation, and to the wider institutional context. The interview data marshalled by Jennifer Platt therefore needs to be treated with some circumspection. It is backed up and related to the archival record, however, and this triangulation makes the story told more convincing.

Conclusion

Halsey's survey of sociology professors yields some interesting data, analysed in chapters 9 and 10 entitled 'Celebrated Sociologists' and 'The Shape of Sociology'. Nevertheless, he urges caution about the limitations of content analysis, quoting Mary Douglas: 'the construction of past times ... has very little to do with the past at all and everything to do with the present' (p. 181). There is an interesting discussion of journals in the field, data on most highly cited sociologists, evidence about the weak hold of quantification on UK sociology, and an extended discussion of the way in which sociology and social policy have become differentiated from one another. It is all very illuminating, but a different sociologist might have presented a different account.

Nonetheless, Halsey's history is a fine piece of work, not least because it is an *interpretation* of the history of British sociology in the twentieth century. Perhaps, to use Howard Becker's analogy about sociological method, it is akin to a mosaic in which different pieces are skilfully fitted together to provide a picture. It is also a measure of how far British sociology has progressed that, as the twenty-first century opens, sociology in Britain has a substantial presence and solid scholarly reputation, represented in one small way by the British Academy conference. Nearly fifty years ago, Edward Shils could write:

> How could sociologists come into existence in Britain when in Oxford and Cambridge sociologists were looked upon as pariahs, as no better than Americans or Germans? How could sociology establish itself as a subject worthy of a freeborn Englishman when it was a product of German abstruseness and American indiscriminateness, when its practitioners in England were often awkward foreigners or restive lower-class boys and girls and when its chief representative was the London School of Economics? (Shils 1985: 168).

We have come a long way since then.

References

Abrams, P. (1968), *The Origins of British Sociology, 1832–1914*, Chicago: University of Chicago Press.

Bannister, R. C. (1987), *Sociology and Scientism: The American Quest for Objectivity, 1880–1940*, Chapel Hill: University of North Carolina Press.

Bannister, R. C. (2003), 'Sociology', in T. M. Porter and D. Ross (eds), *The Modern Social Sciences, vol. 7: The Cambridge History of Science*, Cambridge: Cambridge University Press, pp. 329–53.

Bauman, Z. (1990), *Thinking Sociologically*, Oxford: Blackwell.

Benney, M. (1936), *Low Company, on the Evolution of a Burglar*, London: Peter Davies.

Benney, M. (1966), *Almost a Gentleman*, London: Peter Davies.

Briggs, A. (1961), *Social Thought and Social Action: A Study of the Work of Seebohm Rowntree 1871–1954*, London: Longmans.

Bulmer, M. (1981), 'Sociology and Political Science at Cambridge in the 1920s: An Opportunity Missed and an Opportunity Taken', *The Cambridge Review* 102, 2262 (29 April), pp. 156–9.

Bulmer, M. (ed.) (1985), *Essays on the History of British Sociological Research*, Cambridge: Cambridge University Press.

Carr, E. H. (1961), *What is History?*, London: Macmillan.

Collini, S. (1979), *Liberalism and Sociology: L. T. Hobhouse and Political Argument in England 1880–1914*, Cambridge: Cambridge University Press.

Cowling, M. (1963), *The Nature and Limits of Political Science*, Cambridge: Cambridge University Press.

Elton, G. R. (1967), *The Practice of History*, London: Methuen.

Fleming, D. (1967), 'Attitude: The History of a Concept in America', *Perspectives in American History* 1, pp. 287–365.

Goldthorpe, J. H. (2000), *On Sociology: Numbers, Narratives and the Integration of Research and Theory*, Oxford: Oxford University Press.

Halsey, A. H. (2004), *A History of Sociology in Britain: Science, Literature, and Society*, Oxford: Oxford University Press.

Harris, J. (1977), *William Beveridge: A Biography*, Oxford: Clarendon Press.

Hayward, J., Barry, B., and Brown, B. (eds) (1999), *The British Study of Politics in the Twentieth Century*, Oxford: published for the British Academy by Oxford University Press.

Heimann, J. M. (1998), *The Most Offending Soul Alive: Tom Harrisson and his Remarkable Life*, Honululu: University of Hawai'i Press.

Karl, B. D. (1974), *Charles E. Merriam and the Study of Politics*, Chicago: University of Chicago Press.

Karl, B. D. and Katz, S. N. (1987), 'Foundations and Ruling Class Elites', *Daedalus* 116, 1, pp. 1–40.

Kenyon, J. P. (1983), *The History Men: The Historical Profession in England since the Renaissance*, London: Weidenfeld & Nicolson.

Locke, J. (1960), *Two Treatises of Government: A Critical Edition with an Apparatus Criticus by Peter Laslett*, Cambridge: Cambridge University Press.

Marwick, A. (1970), *The Nature of History*, London: Macmillan.

Platt, J. (1996), *A History of Sociological Research Methods in America, 1920–1960*, Cambridge: Cambridge University Press.

Platt, J. (2003), *The British Sociological Association: A Sociological History*, Durham: sociologypress.

Plumb, J. H. (1969), *The Death of the Past*, London: Macmillan.

Porter, T. M. and Ross, D. (eds) (2003), *The Modern Social Sciences*, Cambridge: Cambridge University Press.

Radzinowicz, L. (1999), *Adventures in Criminology*, Foreword by Lord Woolf, London: Routledge.

Runciman, W. G. (1963), *Social Science and Political Theory*, Cambridge: Cambridge University Press.

Runciman, W. G. (1989), 'Introduction: Confessions of a Reluctant Theorist', in *Confessions of a Reluctant Theorist: Selected Essays*, London: Harvester Wheatsheaf, pp. 1–19.

Shils, E. (1985), 'On the Eve: A Prospect in Retrospect', in M. Bulmer (ed.) (1985), pp. 165–78. (Revised version of an article first published in *The Twentieth Century*, 1960).

Soffer, R. N. (1977), *Ethics and Society in England: The Revolution in the Social Sciences, 1870–1914*, Berkeley, CA: University of California Press.

Soffer, R. N. (1982), 'Why Do Disciplines Fail: The Strange Case of British Sociology', *English Historical Review* 97, pp. 767–802.

Soffer, R. N. (1994), *Discipline and Power: The University, History and the Making of an English Elite, 1870–1930*, Stanford, CA: Stanford University Press.

Taylor, A. J. P. (1965), *English History 1914–1945*, Oxford: Oxford University Press.

Terrill, R. (1973), *R. H. Tawney and His Times: Socialism as Fellowship*, Cambridge, MA: Harvard University Press.

Trevelyan, G. M. (1913), *Clio, a Muse, and Other Essays*, London: Longmans.

Willmott, P. (1985), 'The Institute of Community Studies', in M. Bulmer (ed.) (1985), pp. 137–50.

Wilson, C. H. (1964), *History in Special and in General: An Inaugural Lecture*, Cambridge: Cambridge University Press. Reprinted in C. H. Wilson (1969), *Economic History and the Historian: Collected Essays*, London: Weidenfeld & Nicolson.

Young, M. W. (2004), *Malinowski: Odyssey of an Anthropologist 1884–1920*, New Haven, CT: Yale University Press.

The View from Without

5.
Sociology and History: Partnership, Rivalry, or Mutual Incomprehension?

RODERICK FLOUD & PAT THANE

The 1960s was a period of ferment, intellectual excitement, optimism, and expansion in all the social sciences, including sociology, as Halsey well describes in his book (2004). It is, therefore, an appropriate starting point for a discussion of the relationship between history and sociology in Britain. The ferment affected many younger historians by making them discontented with what they believed to be the limitations of content, method, and theory of their discipline. It affected different branches of history in different ways: political and diplomatic history hardly at all; social and economic history much more.

We both began our careers as working historians in the 1960s and experienced the impact of the developing social sciences on history at that time, though in different ways. Roderick Floud, as a postgraduate student at Nuffield College, was an early proponent of 'cliometrics', the application to historical data of precise quantitative methods drawn from economics. Pat Thane, having also read history at Oxford, went to the LSE as a postgraduate to work with Richard Titmuss to learn about the social sciences, with the intention of moving into contemporary social research. She was gently guided back, to work on a PhD on the history of social policy, by Titmuss and Brian Abel-Smith, who believed that history had an important contribution to make to the social sciences.

The impact of the social sciences on economic history came primarily from neo-classical economic theory allied to econometrics. The economic history of Clapham or Ashton had not, of course, been devoid of theory, but the 'new economic history' put theory at the forefront of the historical discourse; its adherents typically derived a hypothesis from textbooks of economics or from contemporary economists working on a similar topic, gathered evidence—usually quantitative—to test the hypothesis, and based their testing on econometric methods. In this sense, there was little methodological novelty in the early days of the new economic history, since even such apparently novel approaches as 'counterfactual history' derived from such concepts as opportunity cost and from the neo-classical economists' insight that change occurs at the margin.

In social history, change in the 1960s was less dramatic than its young Turks often suggested; it was more diffuse and less easy to identify than the shifts in economic history. This was because the subject matter of social history was broader, as G. M. Trevelyan had pointed out some time before. It is widely believed that Trevelyan characterized social history before the 1960s as 'history with the politics left out'. As with so many oft-recycled quotations, this is not quite what he wrote in the introduction to his *English Social History* (1942). Rather he did write:

> Social history might be defined negatively as the history of a people with the politics left out. It is perhaps difficult to leave out the politics from the history of any people ... But as so many history books have consisted of political annals with little reference to their social environment, a reversal of that method may have its uses to redress the balance ... without social history, economic history is barren and political history is unintelligible. (Trevelyan 1967: 9)

Not quite an endorsement of the 'history with the politics left out' definition.

Trevelyan continued:

> [S]ocial history does not merely provide the required link between economic and political history. Its scope may be defined as the daily life of the inhabitants of the land in past ages: this includes the human as well as the economic relation of different classes to one another, the character of family and household life, the conditions of labour and leisure, the attitude of man to nature, the culture of each age as it arose out of these general conditions of life and took ever-changing forms in religion, literature and music, architecture, learning and thought. (1967: 9–10)

This is a less succinct and memorable definition than that conventionally attributed to Trevelyan, but it characterizes more accurately the work of social historians of his own time and since. For social history was written long before the 1960s. In Britain the work of some prominent economic historians of the 1920s and 1930s, such as R. H. Tawney and Eileen Power (to whose memory Trevelyan dedicated his *English Social History*, describing her as an 'Economic and Social Historian'), was as much concerned with what would now be defined as social history as with strictly economic history. Eileen Power was one of a group of women historians (including Alice Clark and Ivy Pinchbeck) whose work in the inter-war years (such as Power's *Medieval English Nunneries*, 1922, and a number of important essays published after her death as *Medieval Women*) placed and kept women's history—just—on the university syllabuses until the great expansion of this subject area from the late 1960s.

Around the same time in France a similar reaction against history as being primarily the history of political events gave birth to the journal *Annales d'histoire économique et sociale* in 1929. The *Annalistes* aimed to integrate the study of society, economy, politics, intellectual life, geography, and demography, all in their broadest sense, ideally over long time-periods (if sometimes of very small places) in order to understand the complex network of interactions which constitutes a society. This school provided a new rigour both in the definition of social history and its methods. French historians were the first to apply quantitative techniques to the study of politics, social structure, and demography. Driven by *Annales*, social history acquired greater and earlier legitimacy and prominence in French academic life than elsewhere. In Britain it influenced some historians of France, much less those of Britain, before the 1960s.

More important in Britain was historical work from the various strands of the political left which sought to understand social inequality and social institutions historically in order to change them in the present. This broad category encompasses the work of the Hammonds and the Webbs in the early twentieth century; after the Second World War, on the moderate wing, there was G. D. H. Cole (who made important contributions also to sociology) and Asa Briggs; further to the left were the members of the Communist Party History Group who went on to achieve remarkable international eminence — Christopher Hill, Rodney Hilton, Victor Kiernan, E. J. Hobsbawm, and E. P. Thompson.

At the same time Trevelyan's strand of liberal social historiography continued; as an example his research student Jack Plumb, who much admired him, wrote in the 1950s: 'social history, in the fullest and deepest sense of the term, is now a field of study of incomparable richness and one in which the greatest discoveries will be made in this generation' (McKendrick 1975: 15). Between the 1950s and 1970s, Plumb published in both the political and social history of eighteenth-century England. In the 1970s he nurtured among his students a remarkable and varied generation of historians who combined social and cultural with political history, including Roy Porter, John Brewer, Simon Schama, Linda Colley, and David Cannadine.

In 1962 George Kitson Clark's *The Making of Victorian England*, his published Oxford Ford lectures, was dedicated to Trevelyan. Clark declared himself 'primarily a political historian', indeed he was Professor of Constitutional History at Cambridge, but he was 'anxious to write what might be called "history in depth" ', combining demographic, economic, and political history with the study of socio-economic groups at all levels and including central aspects of culture such as religion. This he felt 'quite sure . . . is the right line of development for historiography' (Clark 1962). More influentially, Asa Briggs blended social and political history in his *Victorian People* (1954), *The Age of Improvement* (1959), and *Victorian Cities* (1963).

So when, from the later 1960s, younger historians challenged influential paradigms in the writing of history, at the same time that people were challenging dominant paradigms in other disciplines and outside the academy, they had a wider range of influences to draw upon from within the discipline of history than was always acknowledged. Something was moving before the 1960s. The intellectual ferment among younger historians at this time was therefore not solely influenced by the parallel ferment in the social sciences, though it grew from some of the same roots.

However, historians—not all of them young—did look to the social sciences in the 1960s and 1970s for concepts, theories, and methods which would assist them to reinvigorate the writing of history. In relation to sociology in particular, they did so in ways that varied from the sometimes uncritical application to history of sociological concepts, through a deeply knowledgeable fusion of sociology with history (as in the work of Peter Burke and Michael Anderson, though such expertise was rare), to a profoundly sceptical engagement with the relationship between the two disciplines.

The latter is strongly evident in the introduction to the book which was probably the greatest single influence on the expansion of British social history in the 1960s and 1970s, E. P. Thompson's *The Making of the English Working Class* (1963). Thompson berated in particular the Parsonian, Neil Smelser, and Ralf Dahrendorf for unhelpfully defining class as a 'thing' not a 'relationship' and hence rendering incomprehensible activities in the past which Thompson defined as products of class consciousness. He commented that Dahrendorf's *Class and Class Conflict in Industrial Society* (1963) was 'obsessively concerned with methodology, to the exclusion of the examination of a single class situation in a real historical context' (Thompson 1969 edn: 11). In 1976 Michael Anderson, who started his career in sociology before moving to history, criticized Smelser's *Social Change in the Industrial Revolution* (1959), which was widely read by historians in the 1960s, in similar terms to Thompson though at greater length (Anderson 1976: 317–34).

Anderson took a more positive view of other sociological work, but more striking is how little direct engagement with sociology is evident in the writing of prominent social historians of the 1960s and 1970s, even when one suspects that it exerted at least some unstated influence. Anthropology is more evident, for example, in Gareth Stedman Jones's use of Marcel Mauss's *The Gift* (1954) in *Outcast London* (1971). *The Origins of Modern English Society, 1780–1880* (1969) by Harold Perkin (appointed in the 1960s as the first Professor of Social History in Britain, at Lancaster University) was a challenge to the Marxist or quasi-Marxist paradigm that was so influential among social historians at this time. It defined social history as a 'vertebrate discipline' built around the theme of the history of social structure, rather than as the 'shapeless container for everything from changes in human physique to symbol and ritual' that Hobsbawm perceived (Hobsbawm 1971). Perkin sought to describe and analyse how a 'viable class society', rather than a society defined by conflict, emerged amid the changes of industrialization, but his only direct references to sociology are to Weber and are critical of his 'all-too-famous correlation between capitalism and Protestantism' (Perkin 1969: 13).

This rather combative approach of historians towards sociology is evident in the first issues of two academic journals, both published in 1976, whose appearance demonstrated that social history had firmly arrived as a sub-discipline: *Social History* and *History Workshop.* In an editorial on 'Sociology and History', in *History Workshop*, Gareth Stedman Jones and Raphael Samuel asserted: 'The revival of sociology in post-war Britain . . . has profoundly affected the teaching and study of history', though they cited no examples. The reason, they thought, was obvious: 'the complete vacuum of historical theory'. But they believed:

> [T]he present relationship [between history and sociology] . . . is an unhealthy one and . . . its terms should both be discussed and refined. It leaves the historian in a position of abject dependency, craving recognition and taking theoretical propositions on trust . . . According to some sociologists, this is as it should be: sociologists provide the empty conceptual boxes; it is the humble task of historians . . . to help to fill them.

They considered that 'the pretensions of sociology deserve more critical attention from historians than they have so far received' and they called for historians to enquire into 'the history and claims of sociology . . . to place it historically in the development of bourgeois ideology, whether as a vehicle of bureaucratic utopianism, scientistic fantasy or social fear' (Samuel and Stedman Jones 1976: 6–8).

History Workshop described itself as a 'journal of socialist historians'. It was the most prominent expression of an important socialist strand in the expansion of social history in Britain, which was strongly influenced by the work of E. P. Thompson and, to a lesser extent, of Eric Hobsbawm (who was probably more influential in other countries than in his own). This strand was framed within an often rather understated and untheorized Marxism. Its proponents focused especially upon the history of working and marginalized people in the nineteenth and twentieth centuries. The first ten issues of *History Workshop* contain only three pre-nineteenth-century articles, one by Rodney Hilton, another by Christopher Hill, who were both already very senior. Younger historians of earlier periods are surprisingly absent.

Social History was more broadly representative of the range of work in social history in the 1960s, especially of that before the nineteenth century. The editorial in its first issue stated:

> At the present time, despite the strength of British Marxist historiography and the *Annales* school in France, social history has no orthodox repertoire, no dominant central core . . . no fundamental organizing concept or single

central emphasis. This is a matter of luck rather than management, accident rather than policy. But it is nevertheless a matter for congratulation since it has preserved the many centred character of social history. (Blackman and Nield 1976: 1–3)

The editorial used more moderate language than that of *History Workshop*, but was remarkably similar in its attitude to sociology:

> Many of the methods currently deployed by social historians are broadly derived from social sciences. This process of borrowing poses at least two major problems. Firstly, there are no concepts or methods of social science which may be swallowed whole and applied to historical questions. On the contrary, sociology alone is an intellectual world quite as separate as history, containing as many controversies and contradictory tendencies. Secondly, powerful schools within subjects such as economics or social anthropology . . . have been militantly anti-historical.

The authors detected, and rejected, a tendency to treat

> historical experience as an inert data input, a static object of prior theory. The relation between social history and these social sciences must proceed with caution and on the basis of continuous mutual criticism. *Social History* will encourage this process, but the methods and insights of a sociology or a social anthropology should only be incorporated into historical explanation in such a way that they do no violence to the contextual disciplines of social history.

The editorial boards of these two journals, who presumably endorsed these editorials, included many of the most prominent and the most radical younger social historians of the day. The early issues of *Social History* showed the impact of another important growth area in social history, urban history. Influenced by H. J. Dyos and with inputs both from sociology and geography, urban history provided a structure within which a range of new areas of social history grew and flourished, such as the history of crime, which drew on the radical new sociology of deviance of the 1970s.

Sociology explicitly influenced the work of the Cambridge Group for the History of Population and Social Structure, formed in 1964 by Peter Laslett (an historian of political thought) and E. A. Wrigley (trained as a geographer). Influenced by French rather than British sociology, they set out to apply quantitative techniques developed in France and questions and concepts, previously largely confined to the work of sociologists and anthropologists, to the study of demography and social structure over long time periods (Laslett 1965). The outcome has transformed our understanding of the process of population change (Wrigley and Schofield 1981) and household structure (Laslett and Wall 1972) in Britain over several centuries and has been widely influential elsewhere. But the Cambridge Group also engaged critically with sociology. In the first major publication of the Group, *Household and Family in Past Time* (1972) edited by Laslett and Wall, Laslett commented that neither historians nor sociologists had recently taken an interest in the history of the family, due to 'the relative indifference of social scientists to the time dimension and of historians to the subject matter of the social sciences'. The early work of the Group famously undermined an assumption still routinely taken for granted in sociology textbooks in the 1970s, and beyond, that in 'pre-industrial' society people lived in large extended households which proved incompatible with notionally far more mobile industrial societies. They demonstrated that pre-industrial England was geographically highly mobile and that co-residing households were predominantly small and 'nuclear' rather than large and 'extended'. A similar challenge to sociological assumptions about kinship and the family, from different intellectual origins, came almost simultaneously from Michael Anderson's *Family Structure in Nineteenth Century Lancashire* (1971).

These, however, are rare examples of fruitful engagement between modern social history and sociology. There is a marked contrast between the relationship of social history to sociology and that of economic history to economics. As was mentioned earlier, the 1960s and 1970s were the heyday of what was called, by both its proponents and its detractors, the 'new economic history' or, less often, 'cliometrics'. This movement, which was led from the USA and principally by scholars trained as economists, was devoted explicitly to enhancing historical analysis by the use of the theoretical and statistical tools developed within economics. More specifically, there was a strong focus on a neo-classical approach to micro-economics bolstered by econometric methodologies developed within that tradition. Books and articles written by the new economic historians took pride in displaying their methodological innovations or their borrowings from the writings of contemporary economists, many of whom taught or supervised the graduate students who were at the forefront of the movement. British economic history was an attractive subject to Americans, not only because of the centrality of the experience of the first industrial revolution but because the sources were in English. In addition, many of the American economic historians active in the field had, or soon developed, close links with British universities.

The new economic history was not, of course, universally welcomed. One of its most striking early manifestations, the counterfactual analysis by Robert Fogel of the impact of railroads on the USA, was derided by leading British economic historians when it was first presented to British audiences in the mid-1960s (Fogel 1964). Such historians, who took pride in their separation—in an institutional and personal sense—from economics, argued in terms which were echoed by other historians: the new economic history, they thought, was written in impenetrable jargon, oversimplified the complexity of historical experience and, because of the requirements of econometric and computing methodology, forced the evidence into inappropriate categories. In addition, in terms which recall the similar criticism of sociology by Samuel and Stedman Jones, they deplored the ahistorical character of much economic theory and the lack of training of economists in history and historical method.

Nevertheless, there can be little doubt that economic history was much more influenced between 1960 and 1990 by economics than was social history by sociology. Although books and textbooks continued to be written in less obtrusively theoretical styles, the most successful general summary of modern British economic history (Floud and McCloskey 1981, 1994) was explicitly a product of the new economic history, albeit designed to explain its findings to those with less training in economics and econometrics. The editors acknowledged the hostility which they had encountered:

> This book has been written by economic and social historians who are expert in the use of models and of statistical methods in history, but are conscious of the fears, doubts and misunderstandings which such usage evokes. They wish to show that economic and social history is not diminished thereby but augmented, and that the results can be understood by anyone interested in historical problems. (Floud and McCloskey 1981: xiv)

One reason for the relative success of the new economic history was that it filled what had been essentially a theoretical vacuum. Although the majority of British economic historians, by the 1960s, were probably Keynesians in their analysis of macro-economics, they had no attachment to any school of micro-economics capable of resisting the onslaught of neo-classical economics allied to econometrics. In addition, there was no doubt of the intellectual excitement of the new methods, allied to the opportunities for the analysis of large-scale historical data-sets which were gradually opened up by the spread of computing.

The changes in social history from the 1960s took different forms, which were captured by F. M. L. Thompson's editorial preface to *The Cambridge Social History of Britain, 1970–1950*:

> Economic history ... has ... established its rules of enquiry, its methodologies and its canons of debate ... some might say that it has dug a groove for itself which succeeds in shutting out adequate consideration of factors of central importance, for example the nature and operation of demand and of consumption, in which social history can be illuminating and supportive ...
>
> There may not be a 'new' social history in the same way that there is a 'new' economic history as a school of thought applying econometrics and models drawn from economic theory to the understanding of historical economic phenomena; but social historians draw widely on concepts from historical demography, social anthropology, sociology and political science as well as from economics and are well aware of the importance of quantification. Social historians operating in this conceptually eclectic and experimental fashion do not have the methodological certainty, unity or rigidity of 'new' economic history and deal in conclusions which are probable and plausible rather than directly verifiable. (Thompson 1990)

Certainly between the 1960s and 1990s economic history narrowed in content and in its appeal to young researchers, while social history continued to expand in both respects. For whatever reason the American influence was throughout less evident on social than on economic history. Economic and social history have since moved further apart; social history, which in the 1960s and 1970s placed itself in opposition to political history, came to interact more closely with it, whereas economic history remained remote from political history.

Social history in the 1960s, from whatever perspective it was written, was centrally organized around a conception of society as hierarchically structured, with class as the primary organizing category. In the 1970s and 1980s more historians, like many sociologists, became aware that behaviour and beliefs (about politics for example) could not be explained in terms of socio-economic position as satisfactorily as had been thought. Growing attention to women's history made it clear that gender was also an important social category. Changing ideological preoccupations, combined with a wider academic challenge to structuralism in all its forms, made social historians more sensitive to the variety of divisions within societies and the variety of identities of each individual related to race, nation, age-group, and religion as well as gender and class.

This greatly complicated the writing of social history, as it did that of sociology, leading some to fear that it was about to collapse into random empiricism. Others turned to anthropology for help in understanding social complexity, in particular to the cultural ethnography of Clifford Geertz and the insights of Mary Douglas. The task was further complicated by the growing influence within a wide range of academic disciplines of Foucault and of sociolinguistics, semiotics, and literary theory. The impacts of these very different theories were controversial (Jenkins 1991; Evans 1997; Jordanova 2000). They have had both good and bad effects on historical work, but this is not the place to assess their roles.

Since the 1960s the influence of sociology on social history has been, at best, limited and just one of many theoretical and methodological influences. This perhaps accounts for the increasingly desperate tone of the publications of Peter Burke, one of the few historians consistently over the past twenty-five years to urge historians and sociologists to recognize and build upon their common interests, in particular in his *Sociology and History* (1980) and *History and Social Theory* (1992).

Burke describes, all too aptly, the 'rather crude stereotypes' each group on occasion employs about the other:

> In Britain, at least, many historians still regard sociologists as people who state the obvious in a barbarous and abstract jargon, lack any sense of place and time, squeeze individuals without mercy into rigid categories and, to cap it all, describe these activities as 'scientific'. Sociologists, for their part, have long viewed historians as amateurish, myopic fact-collectors without system or method, the imprecision of their 'data base' matched only by their incapacity to analyse it. In short, despite the existence of an increasing number of bilinguals, . . . sociologists and historians still do not speak the same language. (Burke 1992: 3)

He does not seem convinced that the two disciplines are transcending a 'dialogue of the deaf' (1992: 2–3).

Most of our examples have been drawn from modern history, which we know best. The flagging optimism of Burke, an early modernist, suggests that the relationship between history and sociology is similar among historians of other time periods, that sociology is just one of very many influences even upon social historians. This is suggested also by Paul Cartledge, a historian of ancient Greece, who, less regretfully than Burke, has expressed his belief in the importance of social history and of sociology to it, but does not believe sociology to be the only, or the major, source of relevant theory (Cannadine 2002: 19–35).

We are also less pessimistic than Burke. Social history has been transformed since the 1960s—in the range of its subject matter and in the range of theoretical, conceptual, and methodological tools on which its various branches draw. Where we would differ from Burke, and agree with Cartledge, is in relation to Burke's singling out of sociology as *the* neighbouring discipline with which history should communicate above all; we stress, by contrast, that both the origins and recent development of social history have many sources, of which sociology is only one.

We do, however, argue that history since the 1960s has drawn more on the insights and methods of the social sciences than the social sciences in Britain, including sociology, have drawn on history; this is to the detriment, we would suggest, of scholarship in the social sciences. With distinguished exceptions, notably the current President of the British Academy, the joint editor of this volume (Runciman 1989, 1997), sociology—like the other social sciences—in Britain is notably and sadly ahistorical. There is little sign of the partnership between history and sociology which seemed in prospect forty years ago; rivalry or mutual incomprehension still seems to characterize the two disciplines.

References

Anderson, Michael (1971), *Family Structure in Nineteenth Century Lancashire*, Cambridge: Cambridge University Press.

Anderson, Michael (1976), 'Sociological History and the Working Class Family: Smelser Re-visited', *Social History* 3, pp. 317–34.

Blackman, Janet and Nield, Keith (1976), 'Editorial', *Social History* 1, pp. 1–3.

Briggs, Asa (1954), *Victorian People*, London: Odhams.

Briggs, Asa (1959), *The Age of Improvement, 1783–1867*, London: Longman.

Briggs, Asa (1963), *Victorian Cities*, London: Odhams.

Burke, Peter (1980), *Sociology and History*, London: Allen & Unwin.

Burke, Peter (1992), *History and Social Theory*, Cambridge: Polity Press.

Cannadine, David (ed.) (2002), *What is History Now?*, Basingstoke: Palgrave Macmillan.

Clark, George Kitson (1962), *The Making of Victorian England*, London: Methuen.

Dahrendorf, Ralf (1963), *Class and Class Conflict in Industrial Society*, London: Routledge & Kegan Paul.

Evans, Richard (1997), *In Defence of History*, London: Granta.

Floud, Roderick and McCloskey, D. N. (eds) (1981, 1994), *The Economic History of Modern Britain*, Cambridge: Cambridge University Press.

Fogel, Robert W. (1964), *Railroads and American Economic Growth: Essays in Econometric History*, Baltimore, MD: Johns Hopkins Press.

Halsey, A. H. (2004), *A History of Sociology in Britain*, Oxford: Oxford University Press.

Hobsbawm, E. J. (1971, 1998), 'From Social History to the History of Society', *Daedalus*, reprinted in *On History*, London: Abacus.

Jenkins, Keith (1991), *Re-thinking History*, London: Routledge.

Jordanova, Ludmilla (2000), *History in Practice*, London: Arnold.

Laslett, Peter (1965), *The World We Have Lost*, London: Methuen.

Laslett, Peter and Wall, Richard (eds) (1972), *Household and Family in Past Time*, Cambridge: Cambridge University Press.

Mauss, Marcel (1954), trans. by Ian Cunnison, *The Gift: The Form and Reason for Exchange in Archaic Societies*, London: Cohen & West.

McKendrick, Neil (ed.) (1975), *Historical Perspectives: Studies in English Thought and Society in Honour of J. H. Plumb*, London: Europa.

Perkin, Harold (1969), *The Origins of Modern English Society, 1780–1880*, London: Routledge & Kegan Paul.

Power, Eileen (1922), *Medieval English Nunneries c. 1275 to 1535*, Cambridge: Cambridge University Press.

Power, Eileen (1975), ed. by M. M. Postan, *Medieval Women*, Cambridge: Cambridge University Press.

Runciman, W. G. (1989, 1997), *A Treatise on Social Theory*, 3 vols, Cambridge: Cambridge University Press.

Samuel, Raphael and Stedman Jones, Gareth (1976), 'Sociology and History', *History Workshop* 1, pp. 6–8.

Smelser, Neil (1959), *Social Change in the Industrial Revolution*, London: Routledge & Kegan Paul.

Stedman Jones, Gareth (1971), *Outcast London*, Oxford: Clarendon Press.

Thompson, E. P. (1963, 1969), *The Making of the English Working Class*, London: Victor Gollancz.

Thompson, F. M. L. (ed.) (1990), *The Cambridge Social History of Britain, 1750–1950*, 3 vols, Cambridge: Cambridge University Press.

Trevelyan, G. M. (1942, 1944, 1967), *English Social History: A Survey of Six Centuries, Chaucer to Queen Victoria*, London, Longmans.

Wrigley, E. A. and Schofield, Roger (1981), *The Population History of England, 1541–1871*, Cambridge: Cambridge University Press.

6.
Not Really a View from Without: The Relations of Social Anthropology and Sociology

J. D. Y. PEEL

Asked to give an account of social anthropology's relationship to sociology in Britain under the rubric of 'The View from Without' and being myself as much a hybrid product of the two disciplines as you might find, I begin from the conviction that their histories have been so closely intertwined and overlapping that they cannot really be seen as external to one another at all. We might perhaps see them as cousins or perhaps half-siblings, or (better still) siblings who came to be brought up in different environments, but who still remain in regular contact with one another, and whose resemblances are so close that they are sometimes mistaken for one another. The very strength of Halsey's *History of Sociology in Britain*—that it is so firmly (and necessarily) focused on British sociology's core business, the study of modern Britain itself—is also the source of a certain weakness; but it is a weakness that social anthropologists, and those who have worked on times and places outside modern Britain, have always been on hand to rectify. What can they know of England, who only England know?

As far as their names go, 'anthropology' goes back earlier than sociology, being used in the eighteenth century to denote a philosophical enquiry into human nature, in contrast to theology. 'Sociology', of course, was coined by Comte in the 1830s,[1] in the context of his positivist programme for social and moral reconstruction, and was naturalized in the English-speaking world mainly through the writings of Mill and Spencer. But as the two disciplines

---

[1] For the best recent account, see M. Pickering, *Auguste Comte: An Intellectual Biography* (Cambridge: Cambridge University Press, 1993), vol. 1, pp. 615–24.

are now conceived, they have common origins—recapitulated in most histories—in the social thought of the Enlightenment. This was an enquiry into the character of the emergent, modern society of contemporary Europe, with a view to realizing the conditions for human emancipation from tyranny, ignorance, and poverty. Because this project depended on an understanding of human nature, it was felt to pertain to humanity as a whole, and was thus necessarily comparative as well as historical. The past from which modern Europe had emerged was directly comparable with the present of contemporary non-European peoples, conceptually brought together within the common framework of 'philosophical history' or the 'natural history of society'.

This project remained essentially in place until late in the nineteenth century, though reformulated in more biological terms as a theory of social evolution. By the third quarter of the century, with such works as Tylor's *Primitive Culture* (1871) and Morgan's *Ancient Society* (1877), anthropology began to crystallize as a distinct pursuit, namely as that portion of this project that addressed itself to 'the early history of mankind' (as Tylor's first major book styled it in 1865).[2] As such it was more immediately affected by the implications of Darwin's *The Descent of Man* (1871) than of *The Origin of Species* (1859). Yet it is important that we do not allow the present configuration of academic disciplines to lead us, in retrospect, to find in this period different sets of ancestors for sociology and anthropology.

Yet the anthropology that concerns us, *social* anthropology, was far from being realized when Frazer was appointed to the first chair in it at Liverpool in 1908. What became known as the 'British School' is often dated to 1922: when W. H. R. Rivers (who might perhaps have taken it in a different direction)[3] died, and B. Malinowski and A. R. Radcliffe-Brown published their classic works, respectively *Argonauts of the Western Pacific* and *The Andaman Islanders*. The primary innovation had been in method—the collection of data through a sustained period of intensive fieldwork in a

---

[2] I am much indebted to G. Stocking's two masterly volumes, *Victorian Anthropology* (New York: Free Press, 1987) and *After Tylor: British Social Anthropology 1888–1951* (London: Athlone, 1996).

[3] On Rivers, see R. Slobodin, *W. H. R. Rivers: Pioneer Anthropologist, Psychiatrist of The Ghost Road* (New York: Columbia University Press, 1978).

community—and then, arising from this, that blend of holism and presentism in the mode of explanation that came to be labelled functionalism. This was what was taught in Malinowski's famous seminar at the London School of Economics in the 1920s and 1930s. But it was not until the early 1940s, when Malinowski had left the LSE for Yale and Radcliffe-Brown, having returned from Chicago to the Oxford chair, had taken over its theoretical leadership, that British social anthropology assumed its full distinctiveness (and of which the self-recognition came with the establishment of the Association of Social Anthropologists in 1946). Now its theoretical stance was recast as structural-functionalism, a comparative science of society whose pedigree went back to Durkheim (and, beyond him, Spencer). At this time its typical subject-matter was small-scale societies located within the British colonial empire, particularly in Africa.[4] Its range of concerns and modes of analysis can best be seen in the two collections of papers, *African Political Systems* (eds E. E. Evans-Pritchard and M. Fortes, 1940) and *African Systems of Kinship and Marriage* (eds A. R. Radcliffe-Brown and D. Forde, 1950). It was the publication of this latter volume that led to a remarkable appraisal of British social anthropology in the *American Anthropologist* by G. P. Murdock (who himself generated the Human Relations Area Files project at Yale for the cross-cultural analysis of social structures).[5] While appreciating the British School's ethnographic excellence and analytical penetration, Murdock criticized it for narrowness, neglect of psychology and history, and above all for its virtual abandonment of any use of the concept of culture, the hallmark of American anthropology. So he concluded that what British 'anthropologists' did was not anthropology at all, but a kind of sociology. This view was implicitly confirmed a few years later when the chief paladins of the two disciplines in the USA, A. L. Kroeber and Talcott Parsons, published a short joint paper in the *American Sociological Review* in which they distinguished the domains of anthropology and sociol-

---

[4] On which, see further H. Kuklick, *The Savage Within: The Social History of British Anthropology 1885–1945* (Cambridge: Cambridge University Press, 1991), ch. 5, and J. Goody, *The Expansive Moment: Anthropology in Britain and Africa 1918–1970* (Cambridge: Cambridge University Press, 1995).

[5] G. P. Murdock, 'British Social Anthropology', *American Anthropologist* 53 (1951), pp. 465–73; see further the discussion in Stocking, *After Tylor*, pp. 432–9.

72

ogy as dealing respectively with culture and social structure.[6] As if to corroborate this, there is the curious parallel between the aim of Parsons' social systems theory—to solve the so-called 'Hobbesian problem of order'—and what Gellner once described as the principal discovery of British social anthropology: how order is actually maintained in stateless, segmentary societies.

It is worth elaborating a little on just how much British anthropology's decision to go sociological had separated it from its American cousin. In the USA, the same social-evolutionary origins had been modified by differences both of intellectual tradition and of social context. Its main academic demiurge was Franz Boas, who brought to it the influence of German historical idealism. Debates about the relations of culture and race, history and science, thus became central to it: it became a science of culture, typically as part of the 'four field' approach alongside biology, linguistics, and archaeology. For a long time, its most characteristic subject-matter was native American populations within the USA or elsewhere in North America. At the same time, it developed a discourse of self-vs-other that was highly relevant to questions of identity that mainstream middle America was asking of itself: hence the wide readership gained by the works of such as Ruth Benedict and Margaret Mead, both students of Boas. Indeed, in enabling the analysis of other cultures to serve as a mirror for cultural self-interrogation, American anthropologists may be considered to have revived a tradition of cultural critique that had been practised by Montesquieu and Rousseau. By contrast, the quality product produced by the British School was for export only.

By the early 1950s, British social anthropology had reached its apogee, having gained not just an enviable intellectual coherence, but also (and despite the small number of its practitioners) a high degree of official recognition. It was, in a double sense, a class act.[7] New recruits to the colonial civil service had been receiving anthropological training in Oxford since the 1920s, and there was some continuity in social status from the older generation of

---

[6] A. L. Kroeber and T. Parsons, 'The Concepts of Culture and of Social Structure', *American Sociological Review* 23 (1958), pp. 582–3.

[7] Cf. Donald MacRae, *Ideology and Society* (London: Heinemann, 1961), p. 36: 'The subject, like social work and unlike sociology, has prestige. It is associated with colonial administration—traditionally a career for gentlemen—and entrance into the profession [of social anthropology] . . . confers high status in Britain.'

administrator–anthropologists like Rattray and Amaury Talbot to the new academic professionals. Oxford in fact got its first designated post in 'sociology' in the form of a research lecturership in African sociology held by Evans-Pritchard in the late 1930s. And in the late afternoon of empire in Africa, the sociological expertise of anthropologists was deemed relevant enough to the needs of policy to warrant the establishment of a Colonial Social Science Research Council in 1944, thus pre-dating the all-purpose Social Science Research Council (later ESRC) by over two decades. The Rhodes–Livingstone Institute, founded in 1937 for research on the social problems of 'detribalization' in Central Africa, had brought social anthropology right into the domain of applied sociology, and its success led after the war to the setting up of two further institutes of social research, attached to the new universities at Makerere in Uganda and Ibadan in Nigeria (1947).[8] As with the application of utilitarianism in nineteenth-century India,[9] the British state was often more ready to sponsor policy innovation in the empire than at home.

But alongside the institutional consolidation that the 1950s brought to social anthropology, there was a growing sense of the limitations of its theoretical assumptions, its topics of enquiry, and even its cherished research method. At the same time, as Halsey shows well in his *History*, sociology at the LSE started to acquire the coherence and momentum that would power its lift-off in the 1960s. Philip Larkin's *annus mirabilis* of 1963 might be taken to mark (among other things) the end of this latency period. In that year the Robbins Report gave the green light to the university expansion from which no subject would gain more than sociology; and there occurred the first decennial conference of the Association

---

[8] That at Ibadan was the West African Institute of Social and Economic Research (WAISER), and was mainly headed by an economist, while at Makerere it was the East African Institute of Social Research (EAISR), where anthropology predominated. EAISR was undoubtedly the more successful, largely due to the directorship of Audrey Richards. On Rhodes–Livingstone and EAISR, see further R. Werbner and D. Parkin in R. Fardon (ed.), *Localizing Strategies: Regional Traditions of Ethnographic Writing* (Edinburgh: Scottish Academic Press, 1990), chs 6 and 7 respectively.

[9] E. Stokes, *The English Utilitarians and India* (Oxford: Clarendon Press, 1959).

of Social Anthropologists, at which the discipline recognized the need for new approaches, not least by opening itself to American perspectives. Perhaps no feature of the preceding decade—stretching as it did between India gaining its independence in 1947 and most of Africa by the early 1960s—affected the situation of both subjects in Britain more than the loss of empire: creating difficulties for the one and opportunities for the other. On the one hand, it took away anthropology's accustomed subject-matter and transformed its wider audience, in the forms in which these had been constituted by the relationship between imperial centre and periphery; and on the other, it created a new sense of national self-questioning at home, which at last opened the way for sociology. Complementary to the loss of empire was the growth of Afro-Caribbean and Asian immigrant communities in British cities, an 'other within' that gave British sociology and anthropology a subject-matter of a kind that had engaged both disciplines in the USA for many decades.

In the intellectual and political ferment of the 1960s, sociology had a peculiar centrality, suddenly invested with greater expectations than its institutional and intellectual resources could readily bear. In a celebrated essay, Perry Anderson argued that British culture had an 'absent centre' because, alone of the major European societies, it never produced a classical sociology, a totalizing theory of society developed as a bourgeois response to the critical vision of Marxism.[10] Contrasting this with the theoretical achievement of structural-functionalist anthropology, he then asked why there was even a distinction between the two subjects, since they shared both aims and methods. The distinction lay in their objects. Britain never produced a classical sociology 'largely because [it] was never challenged as a whole from within', so it 'exported its totalization onto its subject peoples. There and only there it could afford scientific study of the theory proscribed at home.'[11] This quasi-Freudian imputation of an impulse to totalization which, checked in its proper sphere, had to find displaced expression elsewhere, may seem a rather odd one for a Marxist theorist to adopt; but it does suggest we need to look more closely at the relations between the two disciplines over the decades in which Britain's anthropology

---

[10] P. Anderson, 'Components of the National Culture', *New Left Review* 50 (1968), pp. 1–56.
[11] Ibid., p. 47.

had blossomed and its sociology faltered. This means very largely at the London School of Economics, which saw the emergence of the one discipline in the 1920s and the eventual consolidation of the other in the 1950s.

Academic sociology in Britain began with the endowment in 1907 of two chairs at the LSE, by a wealthy businessman Martin White: a permanent one occupied by L. T. Hobhouse, whose sociological vision was evolutionist, ethical, and individualist; and a personal chair for Edward Westermarck, who had done fieldwork in Morocco with a strong focus on the evolution of moral ideas.[12] For those who have Spencer down as a founding father of sociology and Tylor of anthropology, it is worth noting that Hobhouse was vehemently opposed to Spencer's anti-statist sociology and at the same time (like Westermarck) strongly influenced by Tylor's 'method of adhesions', a version of which was used in his attempt to establish trends of social development through empirical correlations.[13] The 'anthropological' strand present from the beginning in LSE sociology soon started to separate itself with the appointment of C. G. Seligman, Malinowski's later patron, to a chair in 'ethnology' in 1913. The evolutionary framework which social anthropology all but abandoned in the 1920s formally remained the basis of LSE sociology. In the hands of Hobhouse's long-serving successor in the Martin White chair (1920–54), Morris Ginsberg, it became more philosophical, and its relevance to empirical research on contemporary British society ever more tenuous. But though moribund by the 1950s, its premise that the study of advanced industrial societies and small-scale low-technology societies should be studied within a common framework still informed the LSE's conception of sociology. It underlay the syllabus for the standard course on comparative social institutions, and was kept up into the 1960s by the appointment of specialists in pre-industrial

[12] S. Collini, *Liberalism and Sociology: L. T. Hobhouse and Political Argument in England 1880–1914* (Cambridge: Cambridge University Press, 1979), part III, and Stocking, *After Tylor*, pp. 151–63 on Westermarck, Hobhouse, and the beginnings of sociology/anthropology at LSE.

[13] L. T. Hobhouse, G. C. Wheeler, and M. Ginsberg, *The Material Culture of the Simpler Peoples* (London: Chapman & Hall, 1915).

societies, such as the ancient historian Keith Hopkins.[14] The *British Journal of Sociology*, under Donald MacRae's editorship throughout the 1950s, included social anthropology well within its remit. The Thursday morning seminar on social structure, when I attended it as a graduate student in the mid-1960s, was taken by MacRae and Hopkins among sociologists and by Maurice Freedman and Isaac Schapera among anthropologists. Then there was the formidable presence in the LSE Sociology Department of Ernest Gellner, a philosopher who had taken his PhD in social anthropology—coincidentally, like Westermarck, on Morocco—as 'professor of philosophy with reference to sociology'. While far from being a 'social philosopher' in the Ginsberg mould, Gellner yet revived a kind of philosophical history, in which cross-societal and trans-temporal comparison was flexibly used to yield a penetrating analysis of the cultural and political predicaments of the present.[15]

The renewed interchange between the two disciplines that developed in the 1950s and 1960s was partly a matter of their content (theory, method, and subject-matter), and partly of personnel. On the former, sociologists sought to emulate anthropology's core method, more than its structural-functionalist theory: 'total' fieldwork in local communities. This had already been anticipated in the anthropological inspiration of Mass Observation's research in the late 1930s, but came to full fruition in Michael Young's and Peter Willmot's *Family and Kinship in East London* (1957). Meeting it from the other side was Ronnie Frankenberg's *Village on the Border* (also 1957),[16] Firth's studies of kinship in north London,[17] and a growing number of other studies of local British communities, some of which—like *Coal Is Our Life* (1956)—were the joint work of sociologists and anthropologists.[18] If this was still new for Britain

---

[14] Hopkins went on to hold chairs in sociology at Hong Kong and Brunel universities, before returning to Cambridge to take up the chair of ancient history. His pioneering studies on the demography and social structure of the governing class of the Roman Empire owed much to the work of David Glass.

[15] See especially *Thought and Change* (London: Weidenfeld & Nicolson, 1964), *Spectacles and Predicaments* (Cambridge: Cambridge University Press, 1983).

[16] See Frankenberg's candid and engaging account of how he came to do the project, 'Village on the Border: A Text Revisited' (1989), appended to the 1990 American reprint (Prospect Heights, IL: Waveland Press).

[17] R. Firth and J. Djamour, *Two Studies of Kinship in London* (London: Athlone Press, 1956).

[18] N. Dennis, F. Henriques, and C. Slaughter, *Coal Is Our Life* (London: Eyre & Spottiswoode, 1956).

it was not so in the USA: in his 1966 survey, *Communities in Britain*, Frankenberg made no distinction between sociology and anthropology, tracing his narrative back to the near fusion of the two disciplines in Chicago in the 1930s, and the work of Radcliffe-Brown's protégé Lloyd Warner, who had begun with Australian Aborigines and ended in Yankee City.

Anthropologists' interest in extending their subject-matter from their classic terrain of tribal societies enclosed within the colonial empire was stimulated by the ever more problematic character of research in a decolonizing world, as well as from the demise of evolutionism, which finally released them from the notion that anthropology had to be about 'primitive society' or 'the early history of mankind'. We might see three main ways in which its subject-matter came to overlap more with that of sociology. First, studies of conventionally 'anthropological' topics, like rural communities or kinship and marriage, came to be done 'at home'. Then, fieldwork abroad came increasingly to be done in larger-scale, stratified societies, as in the Mediterranean, the Middle East, and South Asia; and while its settings were still largely rural (as with Adrian Mayer's or F. G. Bailey's studies in India, Paul Stirling's in Turkey, or Edmund Leach's in Sri Lanka),[19] such locally salient phenomena as landlord–peasant relations, local elections, or rural–urban migration required them to address those articulations of state and society which are at the core of so much mainstream sociology. Finally, even on its much worked but still fertile African terrain, anthropology was moving from rural to urban field-sites, where cultural heterogeneity, conflict, and social change demanded attention. The resultant innovations in both methodology (for example statistical sampling, social surveys, the extended case method, etc.) and theory (especially various forms of action theory and transactionalism) moved an anthropology whose paradoxical distinctiveness had lain in its Durkheimian hyper-sociologism closer towards the theoretical eclecticism of British sociology. Here the cardinal figure was Max Gluckman, formerly

---

[19] A. C. Mayer, *Caste and Kinship in Central India* (London: Routledge & Kegan Paul, 1960), followed by *Peasants in the Pacific* (London: Routledge & Kegan Paul, 1961), on Indians in Fiji; F. G. Bailey, *Caste and the Economic Frontier* (Manchester: Manchester University Press, 1957) and *Tribe, Caste and Nation* (Manchester: Manchester University Press, 1960); E. R. Leach, *Pul Eliya—a Village in Ceylon* (Cambridge: Cambridge University Press, 1961); P. Stirling, *Turkish Village* (London: Weidenfeld & Nicolson, 1965).

Director of the Rhodes–Livingstone Institute, appointed in 1949 to head a new department of social anthropology at Manchester, the first outside the Oxford–Cambridge–London triangle. Charismatic and expansionist, Gluckman 'cared little about academic trade-union labels'[20] and saw no aspect or institution of British society—from schools to factories—that might not be grist to the anthropologist's mill.

The meteoric expansion of sociology during the 1960s brought an acute shortage of people to fill senior posts in the new departments, and social anthropologists were often recruited to fill them, particularly those with Rhodes–Livingstone connections, such as John Barnes (Cambridge), Clyde Mitchell (Manchester, later Oxford),[21] and Ian Cunnison (Hull). Peter Worsley, author of a classic study of cargo cults,[22] went to a new chair of sociology at Manchester in what was intended to be a joint department; but Gluckman was such a dominating personality that it is not surprising that sociology soon separated itself, though the two subjects remained fruitfully close. There were other joint sociology–anthropology departments (Swansea, Kent, Hull), as well as some sociology departments that had anthropologists in them because of joint appointments with the new area studies centres set up in the 1960s, as at Birmingham (West Africa), Hull (South-east Asia), or Liverpool and Glasgow (Latin America). There was also a movement the other way. Michael Banton, coming out of LSE sociology, wrote a classic urban ethnography of Freetown;[23] and by the late 1960s completely straddled the two disciplines, serving both as editor of the early volumes of the Association of Social Anthropologists' monograph series (1966), and as the founding editor of the British Sociological Association's new journal *Sociology* (1967). Other professors of sociology had become familiar with anthropological writing through having taught or researched overseas, such as R. P. Dore in Japan, Ilya

---

[20] As Halsey well puts it, *A History of Sociology in Britain* (Oxford: Oxford University Press, 2004), p. 6.

[21] Mitchell had actually first graduated as a sociologist in South Africa (like John Rex), but went on to do a DPhil in social anthropology at Oxford. His final appointment was again in sociology at Nuffield College, Oxford.

[22] P. W. Worsley, *The Trumpet Shall Sound* (London: MacGibbon & Kee, 1957, 2nd edn 1968).

[23] M. Banton, *West African City: A Study of Tribal Life in Freetown* (London: Oxford University Press, 1957).

Neustadt in Ghana, or Stanislav Andreski in Nigeria. Dore held for a time a joint appointment in sociology at the LSE and anthropology at the SOAS, and was critical in the SOAS department adding '... and Sociology' to its title in 1961. A further factor was that in the new universities of the ex-colonial countries, where many anthropologists had worked, academic planners wanted sociology, not anthropology, departments. However unfairly, anthropology was stigmatized as a colonialist, even racist, subject. More cogently, the question was posed: why should there be a different science of society for Africans or Indians than for Europeans or Americans? Anthropologists such as M. N. Srinivas and K. A. Busia, both trained by Radcliffe-Brown at Oxford in the 1940s, eventually assumed chairs of sociology in their home countries, respectively India and Ghana.[24]

All this interchange, both intellectual and personal, between the two subjects had the effect of making British sociology less parochial. While its core activity has always been the analysis of contemporary British society and especially a nexus of topics around class and citizenship, this can hardly be said to amount to sociology unless it is theorized in the light of temporal and spatial otherness. With the demise of the old Ginsbergian paradigm of ethical evolution, which had done something to provide such wider bearings, British sociological theory was largely re-formed in the 1950s through a critical appraisal of such leading American sociologists as Parsons and Merton, Shils and Lazarsfeld; but its comparative and historical range tended to be limited to the societies of Europe and North America as they had developed since the Industrial Revolution. An interest in wider-span comparative traditions was facilitated by British sociology's renewed contact with social anthropology, especially at a time when the latter had its own problems of adjustment to decolonization, the emergence of the Third World, and new agendas for its development. The advance of the social sciences is generated by a complex interplay between their historically evolving subject-matters and a more internal dynamic of ideas. In the 1960s, a turn to history derived from social change in anthropology's ex-colonial fields of research was paradoxically conjoined with the rise of a deeply anti-historical

---

[24] See the photograph in Stocking, *After Tylor*, p. 428.

movement of thought, structuralism, that swept across many disciplines. The counter-pressures were exemplified (if insufficiently addressed) in the ASA monographs on the structural study of myth, and on history and anthropology, which appeared respectively in 1967 and 1968.[25]

Structuralism might be considered a perennial orientation in the human sciences, but its specific roots in linguistics go back to before 1920. Now its main immediate source was the structural anthropology of Lévi-Strauss, which (in contrast to the sociological structural-functionalism of Radcliffe-Brown) shifted the level at which structures were to be analysed from concrete social relations to symbolic systems such as myth, which themselves were taken to express the intrinsic structures of the human mind. Introduced to British anthropology largely by E. R. Leach,[26] it helped to reintroduce culture as an essential part of its subject-matter, and so fed into the rapprochement with American anthropology already under way. Structuralism's impact on sociology was more diffuse, as indebted to literary as to anthropological sources, often mixed with Marxism and 'cultural studies'.[27] But the anthropological structuralist who most influenced British sociology, Mary Douglas, did not derive her vision from Lévi-Strauss, but from a unique blend of influences, including her Catholic formation, fieldwork in the Congo, and Oxford anthropology. Her thought remained strongly sociological, closer to Durkheim and the *Année sociologique* than to Lévi-Strauss.[28] Her pivotal work, *Purity and Danger* (1967), proved to be the most widely read book by a British anthropologist since *The Golden Bough* and at last showed that the classic ethnographies of primitive peoples had vital lessons for the self-understanding of modern industrial societies. Its sequel, *Natural*

---

[25] E. R. Leach (ed.), *The Structural Study of Myth and Totemism* (London: Tavistock, 1967) and I. M. Lewis (ed.), *History and Social Anthropology* (London: Tavistock, 1968), being the papers from ASA conferences held respectively in 1964 and 1966.

[26] See especially his *Lévi-Strauss* (London: Fontana, 1970) and *Culture and Communication . . . An Introduction to the Use of Structuralist Analysis in Social Anthropology* (Cambridge: Cambridge University Press, 1976).

[27] See the influential volume of readings, edited by Essex sociologist Michael Lane, *Introduction to Structuralism* (New York: Basic Books, 1970), and also C. R. Badcock, *Lévi-Strauss: Structuralism and Sociological Theory* (London: Hutchinson, 1975).

[28] R. Fardon, *Mary Douglas: An Intellectual Biography* (London: Routledge, 1999) is the indispensable study.

Symbols (1970), introduced the antithesis of 'grid vs group'[29] and led to a fruitful exchange with the sociologist of education, Basil Bernstein, over his theory of the contrasting speech codes (restricted vs elaborated) of working- and middle-class children. Douglas's wider influence may be gauged from Halsey's finding that, in the 1990s, not only was she was among the ten most cited authors in the three main British sociology journals, but that she was the only anthropologist (and incidentally the only woman too) to be so cited.[30]

But while many sociologists and anthropologists were attracted by the new analytical possibilities offered by structuralism, they were also drawn by external circumstances to address issues of social change. Both disciplines had begun the 1950s dominated by functionalist theoretical paradigms, and anthropological monographs in particular had sought to analyse the operation of functioning systems and used the ethnographic present to describe them. In sociology, the standard charge against functionalism was that it 'could not explain social change'; and so-called 'conflict theories', of which Marxism was taken as the most elaborate example, were widely supposed to be able to do so.[31] Structural-functional anthropology, of course, had a theoretically motivated resistance to historical analysis which sociology, as a discipline holding Max Weber in high esteem, could never have countenanced. In so far as anthropologists now saw their objects of research in dynamic terms, they could not but also ask how the present, in which their enquiries were conducted, related both to the past from which it had emerged and to the future to which all social action is directed. They now had to be responsive to the agendas of local intellectuals in Africa and Asia, who wanted to recover their pre-colonial histories; but it was to be a usable past, one that might serve as a springboard for the development of the new nations. This search for an integral or endogenous path of development often entailed a

---

[29] Though this formulation was original with Douglas, the contrast itself can be traced right back to the Enlightenment origins of both disciplines: the 'grid' perspective on sociality being implicit in Adam Smith's *Wealth of Nations* (1776), while the 'group' perspective is basic to Adam Ferguson's *Essay on the History of Civil Society* (1767).

[30] Halsey, *History*, pp. 178–9.

[31] See the discussion in two deservedly much-used theory texts of the time, John Rex's *Key Problems of Sociological Theory* (London: Routledge & Kegan Paul, 1961) and Percy Cohen's *Modern Social Theory* (London: Heinemann, 1967), esp. ch. 7.

82

critique of distortions brought about by colonialism—and that brought the social-contextual analysis typical of anthropology up against such long-span models of history as the key transitions of classical Marxism or Lenin's theory of imperialism.

The resurgence of Marxism, as much a feature of the late 1960s and 1970s as the rise of structuralism, was much more a response to events in the world than a movement internal to the realm of ideas. The relations between them were complicated, for the battle between structuralism and historicism was waged within Marxism as well as outside it. Three main sources may be distinguished. There was a native British strain, a presence in sociology (though far from dominant there, despite its focus on class and its affinities with the political Left) but bearing its most impressive fruit in the work of such historians as Christopher Hill, R. H. Hilton, and E. P. Thompson. Then there were forms of Marxism current in parts of the Third World, such as dependency theory in Latin America. Finally there was French structuralist Marxism, with Louis Althusser its principal theorist and one of its most influential fields of application in anthropology, in the work of C. Meillassoux, E. Terray, and M. Godelier. As the volume on Marxism from the 1973 decennial ASA conference shows, the interests of social anthropologists were diverse: modes of production and class in lineage-based societies, Marx's concept of ideology as applied to ritual and religion, peasant and petty commodity production in the capitalist periphery.[32] Apart from the group at University College London responsible for the journal *Critique of Anthropology*, the main British conduit of Marxist ideas was Maurice Bloch, whose use of them was critical and selective, not a wholesale appropriation.[33] Some of this anthropological debate about the applicability of Marxist categories to non-capitalist societies was taken into sociology in *Pre-Capitalist Modes of Production* (1975) by Barry Hindess and Paul Hirst. With its exclusively theoretical aim—to mount a radically anti-empiricist critique of any claim of Marxism to be a 'science of history'—it enjoyed an intense if short-lived *succès de scandale* in British sociology (and earned for itself a famous rebuttal by the author of *The Making of the English Working Class*).[34]

---

[32] M. Bloch (ed.), *Marxist Analyses and Social Anthropology* (London: Malaby Press, 1975).

[33] See his *Marxism and Anthropology* (Oxford: Clarendon Press, 1983).

[34] E. P. Thompson, *The Poverty of Theory and Other Essays* (London: Merlin Press, 1978).

Where Marxist concepts, questions, and approaches found a continuing and essential, but not exclusive or always dominant, place was in a new specialism within sociology which emerged in the 1960s: the sociology of development. The figure who did most to launch it was the anthropologist-turned-sociologist Peter Worsley, whose book *The Third World* (1964) went through several impressions and editions, and was followed up two decades later by *The Three Worlds: Culture and World Development* (1984). Grounded upon a mix of mostly anthropological micro-studies and macro-theories drawn from the classical tradition of social theory, its main emphasis was on evolving class structures in relation to various forms of the state, though the Weberian thesis on the role of culture or ideas as factors in social development also came into play.[35] If the core social-structural concept of Africanist anthropology was lineage, as that of British sociology was class, the transit of an anthropologist like Peter Lloyd from his works of the 1950s on Yoruba towns to his 1970s work on class-formation in independent Nigeria tells a clear story.[36] Lloyd's co-workers Gavin Williams and Adrian Peace were prominent in the BSA annual conference whose published papers (1974) marked the definitive recognition of development as a sub-discipline of sociology.[37]

Since the sociology of development dealt with largely agrarian societies, the role of the peasantry was a central theme; and here the work of the Russo-Israeli sociologist Teodor Shanin, who joined Worsley at Manchester, was extremely important.[38] More generally, while it was anthropologists who had so far generated most knowledge of social conditions at the grass roots in developing countries, increasingly the subject-matter of the sociology of development was enlarged by those who were sociologists *de métier*, and

[35] For a review, see J. D. Y. Peel, 'Cultural Factors in the Contemporary Theory of Development', *Archives européennes de sociologie* 14 (1973), pp. 283–303, and a case-study, '*Olaju*: A Yoruba Concept of Development', *Journal of Development Studies* 14 (1978), pp. 135–65.

[36] P. C. Lloyd, *Classes, Crises and Coups: Themes in the Sociology of Developing Countries* (London: MacGibbon & Kee, 1971), and *Power and Independence: Urban Africans' Perceptions of Social Inequality* (London: Routledge & Kegan Paul, 1974).

[37] E. de Kadt and G. Williams (eds), *Sociology and Development* (London: Tavistock, 1974), esp. the two chapters on class: Williams on peasants and Peace on industrial workers.

[38] T. Shanin, *The Awkward Class: The Political Sociology of Peasantry in a Developing Society* (Oxford: Clarendon Press, 1972), and (ed.), *Peasants and Peasant Societies* (Harmondsworth: Penguin Books, 1971).

especially those working outside the ex-colonial areas where most anthropological fieldwork had been done, such as the Middle East, China, and Latin America. Specialists in Latin America[39] were additionally important since so much of the key debates in 'dependency theory' were marked by their Latin American origins and/or reference. A somewhat maverick figure was Stanislav Andreski, who wrote trenchant (and at the time very unfashionable) critiques of developments in Latin America and Africa, laying especial emphasis on the culture and practices of their political classes.[40] It was he, I think, who more than anyone else gave currency to the term 'kleptocracy', since much taken up by African radicals to describe state corruption. I once made some critical comments about Andreski's book on Latin America to Ernest Gellner, who tartly rejoined that it was less a book about Latin America than about pre-war Poland. Some years later, reflecting on Gellner's own theory of nationalism, I felt that his remark went to show that, *mutatis mutandis*, it takes one to know one.[41]

The interests of Gellner and Andreski extended much more widely than the sociology of development: they were part of a notable revival of comparative and historical sociology in the 1970s and 1980s. Anthropologists made significant contributions to it, but its theoretical thrust was more typical of sociology than of anthropology, since it turned more on a Marx–Weber axis of argument than on a Marx–Durkheim one. Gellner's own work in this vein culminated in *Plough, Sword and Book* (1991), with major treatments of Islam and of nationalism—topics that rose rapidly up the scale of public attention in the 1980s[42]—published along the way. At the Marxist end of the spectrum was Perry Anderson's masterly

---

[39] Such as Bryan Roberts at Manchester, Ian Roxborough at the LSE, David Lehmann at Essex and later Cambridge, Maxine Molineux at ILAS (London), John Humphrey at Liverpool and later the IDS (Sussex).

[40] S. Andreski, *Parasitism and Subversion: The Case of Latin America* (London: Weidenfeld & Nicolson, 1966), and *The African Predicament: A Study in the Pathology of Modernization* (London: Michael Joseph, 1968).

[41] Gellner came as a refugee to England from Prague in 1939. His normative parable of Ruritania and Megalomania in *Nations and Nationalism* (1983), pp. 58–62, tells of Czechoslovakia and the Austro-Hungarian Empire.

[42] *Muslim Society* (Cambridge: Cambridge University Press, 1981), *Nations and Nationalism* (Oxford: Blackwell, 1983).

synthetic two-volume study of the origins and demise of feudalism.[43] Though strongly framed within the classic sequence of slavery–feudalism–capitalism, his concern to bring out differences between Western and Eastern variants of European absolutism, and (moving further afield) to assess the standing of Japanese 'feudalism' and 'the Asiatic mode of production' against Western models, implies a distinctly anthropological agenda. And it was a critical consideration of so-called African feudalism, prompted by the faltering of hopes for Africa's development in the 1970s, that inaugurated the mature *œuvre* of Jack Goody, a long-sustained series of comparative studies that began by asking how Africa's institutional baseline differed from those of the agrarian societies of Europe and Asia. The scope of Goody's comparisons ramified over agriculture, war and the state, technology, marriage and property, writing and literacy, cuisine, and many other topics.[44] Another Cambridge anthropologist (and social historian), Alan Macfarlane, developed a related line of argument about the distinctive conditions of English society and development, again making heuristic use of comparisons between West and East.[45]

The appeal of Marxism peaked sometime in the late 1970s and the theoretical tenor of comparative macro-sociology thereafter shifted in a Weberian direction. This is most evident in Michael Mann's *The Sources of Social Power* (vol. 1, 1986), both in his treatment of the sources of power as plural (economic, political, ideological, and military), and in his configuration of the world-historical story: a period of 'general social evolution' giving way to civilizations and then empires, from which emerge the world religions—Weber's original 'cultural switchmen'—to provide the pivot of the narrative, before it homes in on 'the European dynamic'. Mann (who began in the thematic heartland of British

---

[43] P. Anderson, *Passages from Antiquity to Feudalism* and *Lineages of the Absolutist State* (both London: New Left Books, 1974).

[44] J. Goody, *Technology, Tradition and the State in Africa* (1971), *Production and Reproduction: A Comparative Study of the Domestic Domain* (1976), *The Domestication of the Savage Mind* (1977), *Cooking, Cuisine and Class: A Study in Comparative Sociology* (1982), *The Logic of Writing and the Organization of Society* (1986), *The Oriental, the Ancient and the Primitive: Systems of Marriage and the Family in the Pre-Industrial Societies of Eurasia* (1990), *The Culture of Flowers* (1993). All these published at Cambridge by Cambridge University Press.

[45] A. Macfarlane, *The Origins of English Individualism* (Oxford: Blackwell, 1978), *The Culture of Capitalism* (Oxford: Blackwell, 1987), *The Savage Wars of Peace: England, Japan and the Malthusian Trap* (Oxford, Blackwell, 1997).

sociology, with the analysis of class)[46] was drawn to the 'anthropological' topic of religion by its evident importance in pre-modern and non-European societies; and of all sociologists, it is those of religion who perhaps are most likely to want to compare the exceptionally secular character of modern Europe—but not, of course, the USA—with other societies where religion is still of pervasive force.

Both the two senior sociologists of religion began from studies of the cultural margins of British life: Bryan Wilson on sectarianism and David Martin on pacifism.[47] Later they engaged in a vigorous debate about the extent and significance of secularization in Europe.[48] Both moved on to comparative studies of religious movements in the Third World. Wilson's *Magic and the Millennium* (1973) drew on a vast, mainly missionary and anthropological, literature on the cargo cults, prophet movements, and charismatic churches that had emerged in response to the colonial impact in Africa, the Pacific, and the Americas.[49] His analysis, in anticipating a 'rational mutation of religious responses', echoed in Weberian terms those Marxists like Worsley who had analysed such movements as essentially transitional phenomena. With a fine implicit irony, Martin's project, conceived two decades later and reflecting the new saliency of religion in the age of globalization, took one of the sectarian orientations that Wilson had treated in his 1959 study of Britain—Pentecostalism—and explored how it had become the most dynamic force in world Christianity, first in Latin America and then in a wider comparison.[50] Martin's studies have been a major

[46] M. Mann, *Consciousness and Action among the Western Working Class* (Cambridge: Cambridge University Press, 1973).

[47] B. R. Wilson, *Sects and Society: The Sociology of Three Religious Groups in Britain* (London: Heinemann, 1959); D. A. Martin, *Pacifism: An Historical and Sociological Study* (London: Routledge & Kegan Paul, 1965).

[48] B. R. Wilson, *Religion in a Secular Society: A Sociological Comment* (London: Watts, 1966); D. A. Martin, *A General Theory of Secularization* (Oxford, Blackwell, 1978).

[49] For an extended critical appraisal, see J. D. Y. Peel, 'An Africanist Revisits *Magic and the Millennium*', in E. Barker, J. A. Beckford, and K. Dobbelaere (eds), *Secularization, Rationalism and Sectarianism: Essays in Honour of Bryan R. Wilson* (Oxford: Clarendon Press, 1993), pp. 81–100.

[50] D. A. Martin, *Tongues of Fire: The Explosion of Protestantism in Latin America* (Oxford: Blackwell, 1990), and *Pentecostalism: The World Their Parish* (Oxford: Blackwell, 2002).

point of reference for anthropologists working on 'fundamentalism' within different world religions.[51]

The pattern of interchange between social anthropology and sociology, that evolved between the 1950s and 1980s, rested upon the historic intellectual prestige of the former and the growing institutional strength of the latter, on the openness of British sociology to an anthropology that conceived of itself as essentially sociological, and on the reciprocal tendency of both subjects to move into one another's territories: of anthropology to 'come home', and of sociology to move abroad, taking development as one of its specialisms. Yet this did not lead to the fusion that some predicted— rather the reverse, at least institutionally. Departments that combined both subjects tended to divide as they got bigger. As the numbers of qualified sociologists grew, it became less and less necessary to turn to anthropologists to fill sociology chairs. The 1980s brought new institutional pressures to bear. The Thatcher government's hostility to the social sciences for their supposed deficiencies in both scientific rigour and public utility led to sharp reductions in levels of funding—equally for research, studentships, and academic posts. The new outlook was signalized in the rechristening of the SSRC as the Economic and Social Research Council, and its reorganization to reduce the influence of the disciplines, as defined by their academic practitioners, in favour of government-led research priorities. While there is no doubt that sociology bore the brunt of official opprobrium, social anthropology was probably more adversely affected by the changes. As a small discipline whose subject-matter tended to the exotic, the loss of its own SSRC committee undermined its ability to promote its disciplinary priorities in the allocation of research grants; and, having lost its former usefulness for colonial administration, it found it less easy than sociology to respond to the new utilitarianism of 'Why should the British taxpayer fund this?' The pressure to focus

---

[51] See, for example, Susan Bayly, 'Christianity and Competing Fundamentalisms in South Indian Society', in M. Marty and R. S. Appleby (eds), *Accounting for Fundamentalisms* (Boston, MA: Beacon, 1994), or A. Corten and R. Marshall-Fratani (eds), *Between Babel and Pentecost: Transnational Pentecostalism in Africa and Latin America* (London: Hurst, 2001).

research on topics with a clear relevance to British economic and social policy fostered the reduction, not just of social anthropology as a strand within sociology departments, but also of the sociology of other times and places more generally: the sociology of development began to lose its appeal, and those sociologists who worked on developing countries tended to become somewhat marginal within their departments.

The demand to be 'relevant' and 'useful' affected social anthropology too. One path to relevance was to move closer to home. The Celtic regions of the British Isles and the 'honour-and-shame' zone of the Mediterranean had for decades been deemed sufficiently 'other' to merit anthropological attention, but now a growing number of anthropologists found research topics in Britain, or at least in Europe.[52] From the mid-1980s, and even more after the collapse of the Soviet Union in 1991, Eastern Europe and 'post-socialist societies' emerged as important new fields for anthropology.[53] Aside from the perfectly valid intellectual reasons for including Europe within anthropology's remit, this shift of focus was also strongly driven by such practical considerations as decreased research funding, less availability of the extended leave which overseas fieldwork requires, and the increasing difficulty or even impossibility of carrying out research in many Asian and African countries. While anthropologists-at-home came to have much to say on diverse domestic issues—from child abuse to the new reproductive technologies[54]—overseas anthropology was best able to demonstrate its relevance to policy in the field of development. The 1980s saw a gradual shift from an older conception of 'applied anthropology' towards a new specialism, 'anthropology of development', for which professional opportunities opened up within

[52] See A. Jackson (ed.), *Anthropology at Home* (London: Tavistock, 1987), papers from the 1985 ASA conference on this theme. For figures, see A. Kuper, *Anthropologists and Anthropology* (rev. edn, London: Routledge & Kegan Paul, 1983).

[53] Among British anthropologists, C. M. Hann was the key pioneer of this field: see his edited volumes *Socialism: Ideals, Ideologies and Local Practice* (London: Routledge, 1993), an ASA monograph, and *Postsocialism: Ideals, Ideologies and Practices in Eurasia* (London: Routledge, 2002).

[54] J. S. La Fontaine, *Speak of the Devil* (Cambridge: Cambridge University Press, 1998); J. Edwards, S. Franklin, E. Hirsch, and M. Strathern, *Technologies of Procreation* (Manchester: Manchester University Press, 1993).

the context of international aid projects.[55] Though there was some work which straddled the divide between them,[56] this 'anthropology' came to differ from 'sociology' of development in being less concerned with macro-historical processes of change and more with what actually happens on the ground in development projects. Here it aimed to bring the critical potential of anthropology's own speciality—detailed ethnography—to bear, not just on the people of the poor South who are the target of development interventions, but also on the NGOs and governmental and international agencies that do the intervening.

As the same time as institutional pressures led more anthropologists to find research topics at home (and so to move further into a terrain well populated by sociologists), the two disciplines were also affected by a new intellectual current with a counter potential: to bring sociology over towards a theoretical terrain much more familiar to anthropology, namely culture.[57] British anthropology's reserve towards the concept of culture had by now been fairly well laid to rest. After structuralism, there was a new interest in problems of meaning, semantics, and local systems of knowledge.[58] At Oxford, the Institute of Social Anthropology's addition of '. . . and Cultural' to its name in 1990 (though there were local administrative reasons for the change) seemed to carry a wider message. 'Culture theory' was what Mary Douglas came to call her distinctive line of work. But insofar as sociology too turned towards cultural analysis, a much greater influence than anthropology's came from a hybrid quasi-discipline which grew up between them: 'cultural studies'. A remarkable feature of the genealogy of cultural studies in Britain is that the literary scholars who founded it were so ignorant of, or indifferent to, either sociology or anthropology. Richard Hoggart's *Uses of Literacy* (1958) is often praised for the

---

[55] See R. Grillo and A. Rew (eds), *Social Anthropology and Development Policy* (London: Tavistock, 1985), based on papers given at the 1983 decennial conference of the ASA.

[56] P. Worsley (ed.), *Two Blades of Grass: Rural Cooperatives in Agricultural Modernization* (Manchester: Manchester University Press, 1971), N. Long, *An Introduction to the Sociology of Rural Development* (London: Tavistock, 1977), and A. F. Robertson, *An Anthropology of Planned Development* (Cambridge: Cambridge University Press, 1984).

[57] See especially Z. Bauman, *Culture as Praxis* (London: Routledge, 1973, new edn 1999).

[58] E.g. D. Parkin (ed.), *Semantic Anthropology* (London: Tavistock, 1983). The 1993 decennial conference of the ASA took as its theme 'The Uses of Knowledge: Global and Local Relations'.

90

'ethnographic' quality of his description of the urban Yorkshire working-class milieu of his origins—and it is a pretty functionalist ethnography at that[59]—but his ethnographic approach does not seem to have owed anything to anthropological models. Raymond Williams's *Culture and Society 1780–1950* (1958), the initiating theoretical influence on cultural studies, is astonishingly bereft of reference to the pioneer social-scientific theorists of society and culture—Spencer, Tylor, etc.—who were the contemporaries of the novelists and literary essayists whose work he considers.[60] It was Stuart Hall who both led cultural studies to more 'sociological' topics—deviancy, race and ethnicity, state and nation, the mass media—and redirected its theoretical agenda in the light of structuralism, anthropological, and otherwise. 'Ethnography' came to be a primary genre within cultural studies, and a collection like *Resistance through Rituals*, which picks up on a classic anthropological theme, fed back into mainstream anthropology.[61]

Simultaneous movements of convergence and divergence continue to mark the relations of sociology and social anthropology. The convergences, whether in method or in theoretical orientation, are most evident in those fields tilled by both disciplines, such as ethnicity, youth and gender, diasporic communities, and topics around culture and communication, where it is often difficult to tell whether authors are sociologists or anthropologists. Globalization, 'nation and narration', identity, embodiment, processes of subjectification are prominent themes common to both. There may be certain contingent contrasts as regards particular topics. In the study of ethnicity in Britain, for example, anthropologists have mainly focused on the Asian population, with a concern for cultural difference, while Afro-Caribbeans have drawn more attention from sociologists, who have been more oriented to social policy issues,

[59] Graeme Turner, *British Cultural Studies* (London: Routledge, 1990, 3rd edn 2003), p. 39, writes of his 'admirable . . . sense of cultural connectedness . . . an organic, rather than a constructed, culture'.

[60] And sometimes close intellectual associates: see N. Paxton, *George Eliot and Herbert Spencer: Feminism, Evolutionism and the Reconstruction of Gender* (Princeton, NJ: Princeton University Press, 1991).

[61] Cf. the influence of S. Hall, T. Jefferson, and B. Roberts (eds), *Resistance through Rituals: Youth Subcultures in Post-War Britain* (London: Hutchinson, 1976), on Jean Comaroff's *Body of Power, Spirit of Resistance: The Culture and History of a South African People* (Chicago: Chicago University Press, 1985).

such as racial discrimination.[62] Even so, it was an anthropologist, Kenneth Little, who inaugurated the study of Black Britons;[63] and it is to be expected that any emergent division of labour between the disciplines will soon be blurred, since it lacks any rationale of either theory or method.

As regards theory and methods it is hard to find any hard-and-fast divide; rather, the differences between the two subjects are not fixed and categorical, but shifting and distributional. Major points of theoretical reference—such figures as Bourdieu and Foucault—tend to be largely shared. Ethnography, which is usually considered by anthropologists as their essential and self-defining research method, is widely practised by sociologists. The 'multi-sited ethnography' that anthropologists often call for in today's age of globalization actually has its most notable early precedent back in Chicago sociology, in the classic study by Thomas and Znaniecki of Polish peasant migrants. In contrast, though anthropologists have made extensive use of statistical techniques and worked with large data-sets, this kind of work, associated with a 'positivist' programme for social science, is obviously much more typical of sociology. Yet the real point is not that social anthropology has come to see itself more exclusively as a hermeneutic discipline, in contrast to sociology, but that the antinomy between causal/scientific and interpretative approaches to the understanding of social action is a theoretical dilemma common to both disciplines.

The understandable concern of anthropologists that their smaller and (in a climate of ceaseless underfunding and rationalization) more vulnerable subject should not be swallowed up by its larger relative leads them to strategies both institutional and intellectual. In order to put some space between the two subjects—for reasons that we know well from Simmel—the social anthropologists in the British Academy opted to be go in with human geography rather than sociology when the old Social Studies section was divided in 1994, and when Oxford University reorganized itself into five divisions in 2000, its social anthropologists went with their biological fellows into life and environment sciences rather than

---

[62] M. Banks, *Ethnicity: Anthropological Constructions* (London: Routledge, 1996) pp. 97–8, citing the Cambridge anthropologist Susan Benson (who is herself an exception to the rule).
[63] K. Little, *Negroes in Britain: A Study of Racial Relations in English Society* (London: Kegan Paul, Trench, and Trubner, 1947).

with the sociologists into social sciences. The intellectual rationale for such distancing is more problematic, though the protean nature of anthropology, over the two centuries of its existence, offers various possibilities. The most obvious strategy has been simply to seek to replace society with culture as anthropology's theoretical object, as was surely implicit in the motion 'The concept of society is theoretically obsolete', carried at a meeting of the Group for Debates in Anthropological Theory in 1989.[64] But this was but a gesture: a year later, society was back as the key theme at the first meeting of the new European Association of Social Anthropologists, which called its new journal *Social Anthropology* (no doubt in part to distinguish it from what the Americans do).[65] Another option is for anthropology to emphasize its links with archaeology, but that must make it seem that it is still essentially about the early history of mankind. The most far-reaching strategy is to revive the original conception of anthropology as the science of man, rather than of society: its subject-matter 'human nature'. This implies somehow positioning itself at the centre of 'the human sciences' (including human biology, genetics, psychology, demography, and, of course, sociology) and, more specifically, even recasting itself again more within an evolutionary framework. The socio-biology of the 1970s had been virtually ignored in British social anthropology, but the idea that anthropological analysis should be grounded in cognitive psychology now began to attract significant attention.[66] Yet even this development might equally be extended to sociology (though there this is even more of a minority concern): W. G. Runciman, who has long advocated a neo-Darwinist framework for sociology, has always treated sociology and social anthropology as essentially branches of the same subject.[67] That has been my view too.

---

[64] See T. Ingold (ed.), *Key Debates in Anthropology* (London: Routledge, 1996), pp. 55–98. The motion was proposed by Marilyn Strathern and Christina Toren, and opposed by J. D. Y. Peel and Jonathan Spencer.

[65] A. Kuper (ed.), *Conceptualizing Society* (London: Routledge, 1992).

[66] For example, P. Boyer, *Religion Explained: The Human Instincts that Fashion Gods, Spirits and Ancestors* (London: William Heinemann, 2001), and H. Whitehouse, *Modes of Religiosity: A Cognitive Theory of Religious Transmission* (Walnut Creek, CA: AltaMira Press, 2004).

[67] W. G. Runciman, *The Social Animal* (London: HarperCollins, 1998). See too his *A Treatise on Social Theory, vol. 1: The Methodology of Social Theory* (Cambridge: Cambridge University Press, 1983) which throughout addresses its prescriptions equally to 'sociologists, anthropologists and historians' (pp. 55, 332, 337).

7.
Demography's British History and its Relation to Sociology

JOHN ERMISCH

This essay attempts to complement on a small scale Professor Halsey's *A History of Sociology in Britain*. It outlines the development of demography in Britain, and examines its links with the development of British sociology. As will become clear, there is a particularly strong link in the person of David Glass, a towering figure in British demography and a pioneer in British sociology. He also represents a personal link, because he was the editor who accepted my first demographic paper for publication just before his death. By chance, it appeared in the issue of *Population Studies* containing a memoir of Glass by the late Eugene Grebenik, another shaper of the history of demography. I am unable to bring to this essay first-hand knowledge similar to that of Professor Halsey, but I have drawn heavily on this memoir and Grebenik's history of demographic research in Britain.[1] A 'view from economics' is also represented, because that is the discipline in which I was trained and through which I approach demographic studies. Also, much early interest in population came from economists.

Before the start of the twentieth century, demography was mainly the study of mortality. William Farr, who created Britain's system of vital statistics, was primarily interested in mortality, including the relation between mortality and social factors. Thanks to Farr and his successors, Britain had one of the most comprehensive systems of mortality statistics at the time; techniques of mor-

---

[1] E. Grebenik, 'David Victor Glass (1911–1978)', *Population Studies* 33 (1979), pp. 5–17, and E. Grebenik, 'Demographic Research in Britain, 1936–1986,' *Population Studies* 45 (1991), Population Research in Britain Supplement, pp. 3–30.

94

tality measurement and life table construction had been perfected by the end of the nineteenth century; and the development of mortality was reasonably well documented and understood. Less was known about fertility and marriage, but interest in them was growing, partly in consequence of the decline in the crude birth rate from the 1870s and concerns about the 'quality' of the population. Questions relating to the fertility of married women were included in the 1911 Population Census, and the subsequent analysis of these data established the existence of a fertility differential between social groups, confirming studies in Karl Pearson's Eugenics Laboratory at University College during the early years of the twentieth century.

Economists took an early interest in population issues, although generally not in terms of detailed statistical analysis. The obvious forerunner was Thomas Malthus's *First Essay on Population* (1798), and modifications by Nassau Senior in his *Two Lectures on Population* (1831) were influential during the nineteenth century. Around the start of the twentieth century, Edwin Cannan made contributions to understanding factors affecting the size of the population. Harold Wright published *Population* in the Cambridge Economic Handbooks series in 1923, which followed a small book a year earlier by Harold Cox called the *Problem of Population*. These and other publications by economists during the 1920s, including Sir William Beveridge and John Maynard Keynes, were less concerned with the determinants of population growth and more with its effect on the economy.

There were no university posts in demography before 1938, with the possible exception of the chair in epidemiology and vital statistics at the London School of Hygiene. According to Grebenik,

> the only instruction on population questions was normally provided for students of economics . . .
>
> In general, at the time [1918–38], the study of human population was regarded as being primarily a subject for biologists. The only work published in the English language on population at the time was A. M. Carr-Saunders's *The Population Problem*, which appeared in 1922 and which drew heavily on anthropological sources in considering population growth at different stages of human evolution. (Grebenik 1991: 4)

As Director of the LSE, Beveridge obtained a Rockefeller grant to extend 'the natural base of the social sciences', and it was used to establish a chair of social biology at the LSE. In 1930, Lancelot Hogben was appointed to it. He brought together a number of people interested in demography, among them R. R. Kuczynski, Enid Charles, and David Glass. Kuczynski, a German refugee scholar, had pioneered the use of gross and net reproduction rates in population analysis and, when Hogben left the LSE in 1937, he was appointed to a university readership in demography at the LSE, the first post specifically designated in demography in a British university. Glass graduated from the LSE in 1932 as a geographer, and served as Research Assistant to Beveridge in a research project on family life. His interest in population problems grew out of this post and his association with Hogben and his colleagues, to whom he often expressed his intellectual indebtedness.

In Grebenik's view: 'The work of Hogben and his group was instrumental in distancing the study of population from eugenics and to give it an independent status of its own' (1991: 8). We can obtain a flavour of their work from the symposium volume, *Political Arithmetic*, edited by Hogben and published in 1938. It contained historical studies of the development of fertility and mortality, population projections, and a section dealing with the relationship between intellectual ability and educational opportunity, a subject that has a close connection with the subsequent interests of sociologists and that David Glass would return to after the war.

A very important institution in the history of British demography is the Population Investigation Committee (PIC). Professor Carr-Saunders, who succeeded Beveridge as Director of the LSE in 1937, was one of the major influences behind its foundation. In his 1935 Galton lecture to the Eugenics Society, he bemoaned the relative neglect of numerical studies by those interested in eugenics. In response, the Society decided in 1936 to set up the PIC, and provided financial support for it for another decade. The PIC became the principal centre for population research in Britain during the next twenty-five years. According to Grebenik (1991: 9), its success was due to three men: Carr-Saunders, who served as its Chairman for twenty years, C. P. Blacker, who served as its Honorary Secretary for nearly forty years, and David Glass, who was appointed its first Research Secretary. In his role as its Research Secretary from its foundation until 1948, David Glass established the PIC's reputation. During the late 1930s, he focused on the study of population policies, culminating in the publication of his doctoral thesis, *Population Policies and Movements in Europe*, a book that remains a classic.

Another important (if temporary) institution in the development of demographic research in Britain was the Royal Commission on Population, which was set up in 1944. The PIC was well represented in its activities. Its members included Sir Alexander Carr-Saunders. While not a member of the Commission, David Glass served on the Statistics Committee and the Biological and Medical Committee, set up to advise the Commission. Also, R. R. Kuczynski was a member of the Statistics Committee and C. P. Blacker a member of the Biological and Medical Committee. There was also an Economics Committee, chaired by Hubert Henderson and including among its five members W. B. Reddaway, who had published his *Economics of a Declining Population* in 1939.

David Glass wrote a series of memoranda for the Commission and its committees, and together with Kuczynski he was the driving force behind the Family Census of 1946 (a 10 per cent sample of the female population), and also the large-scale survey of contraceptive practice carried out on behalf of the Biological and Medical Committee by Dr Lewis-Faning. The Family Census was the largest enquiry of its kind in Britain since the 1911 Census. Grebenik joined the Secretariat of the Commission in 1945 as assistant director of the Family Census. It was the first time that fertility was analysed on a cohort rather than a period basis, and David Glass devised a new categorization of social groups. While the Family Census was successfully organized in less than a year and the Royal Commission used preliminary results for its report, the full analysis took much longer than expected. Glass and Grebenik published their final report on the analysis in 1954.[2] The Family Census of 1946 served as a model for the fertility component of the 1971 Census. The Lewis-Faning enquiry was the first of several designed to measure the prevalence of contraceptive practice.

Another member of the Royal Commission's Secretariat was John Hajnal, who began his distinguished career there. He improved understanding of population dynamics, and his work on

---

[2] D. V. Glass and E. Grebenik, *The Trend and Pattern of Fertility in Great Britain: A Report on the Family Census of 1946* (2 vols, London: HMSO, 1954).

population projections with W. A. B. Hopkin showed that some of the alarmist pre-war projections were unfounded.

In 1945, David Glass was appointed Reader in Demography at the LSE, a post which had been vacant since Kuczynski's retirement in 1941. He brought the PIC with him to the LSE, where it has remained, although it is formally independent of the School. He became Chairman of the PIC when Carr-Saunders retired, and he held that office until his death in 1978.

One of the earliest research activities of the PIC after the war was a study of the services available to women during pregnancy and childbirth and of the costs of childbirth. Its associates in this study were the Royal College of Obstetricians and Gynaecologists and the Society of Medical Officers of Health. The three bodies appointed a joint committee, which included C. P. Blacker and R. M. Titmuss among its members, with David Glass as the Secretary. All mothers who gave birth in Britain during a week in March 1946 constituted the study population. Dr J. W. B. Douglas was appointed to direct the study, and its first publication, *Maternity in Britain*, was in 1948. But the path-breaking nature of this study only begins here. Largely as a result of Glass's initiative, the food rationing system and national registration were used to trace a sub-sample of children until they began school and subsequently to follow their school careers. As research-users of the so-called 'Douglas cohort' are aware, this turned out to be the longest running longitudinal survey on health and development to be conducted anywhere. It provided a model for the National Child Development Survey ('1958 birth cohort'), the 1970 Birth Cohort Study, and the Millennium Cohort Study.

Another development closely following Glass's readership appointment was the foundation of the journal *Population Studies* in 1947. There was only one other demographic journal in the English language at that time, *Population Index* published in Princeton, which was primarily a bibliographic journal. *Population Studies* remains one of the two top demographic journals in the world, along with *Demography*, published in the USA. Glass was Editor of *Population Studies* from its foundation until his death in 1978, and Grebenik was also associated with it since its beginning; first as an editorial assistant, then Joint Editor and then Editor after Glass's death. In that role, both made a major contribution to shaping the field of population studies and demography, not just in Britain, but internationally. In 1997, Grebenik was awarded (jointly with Joel Cohen) the first Olivia Schieffen Nordberg Award 'for excellence in writing and editing in the population sciences'.

Grebenik contributed to the development of international demography in other ways as well. After graduating with first class honours in economics from the University of London in 1938, he was appointed assistant lecturer at the LSE in 1940, being promoted to lecturer in 1944 and to Reader in 1949, the year in which he began his long association with the International Union for the Scientific Study of Population (IUSSP). He was Secretary-General of the Union from 1963 to 1972, during which time he organized three IUSSP General Population conferences. He was appointed Professor of Social Studies at the University of Leeds in 1954, where he remained until taking up appointment as the first Principal of the newly established Civil Service College in 1969.

Glass was appointed to a chair in sociology at the LSE in 1948, and one of the first major projects he initiated as Chair was a study of social mobility in Britain. The techniques used in the study were indebted to demography, and it harks back to Hogben's *Political Arithmetic* symposium. As detailed in Professor Halsey's book, sociologists were to follow in studies of social mobility, although not necessarily with Glass's blessing.

To sum up Glass's contribution, I quote from Grebenik:

> David Glass's importance in furthering the teaching of and research in demography during the 20 years following the war cannot be overestimated. On the teaching side, he was responsible for the introduction of demography as an optional subject in the new honours degree in Sociology which was begun in 1953. The subject was also available as an option to students reading for the B.Sc.(Econ) degree . . . To the best of my knowledge these were the only courses then available in British universities in which undergraduates could study the subject. (Grebenik 1991: 19)

Ample evidence of his pioneering role in demographic research and in developing the subject has already been presented.

By the 1950s, demographers' interests had moved to the situation in developing countries. Increasing attention was devoted to devising methods to obtain reliable estimates of birth and death rates and trends in the size and structure of population in countries in which births and deaths are not recorded. William Brass, who was at the time working at the East African Statistical Department, showed how these could be derived from simple questions on censuses and surveys. His first papers, in 1953 and 1954 in *Population Studies*, showed how it was possible to derive fertility rates from restricted data on reproductive histories and ratios of total to first births. This line of research has been extended and developed by Brass, his students, and others. Much of our knowledge about the demography of Asia, Africa, and Latin America has been acquired through the use of these methods, which he called 'indirect estimation', but what most demographers call 'Brass estimates'.

Brass returned to the UK in 1955, first to the Department of Statistics in the University of Aberdeen, where he remained until 1964. During this period, he took a year's leave of absence at the Office of Population Research at Princeton University. From his collaboration there with Ansley Coale and others came *The Demography of Tropical Africa*, which remained the definitive statement on the subject for well over a decade. In 1965, he became the London School of Hygiene and Tropical Medicine's first demographer, first as a Reader and then as Professor of Medical Demography from 1972 until his retirement in 1988. In 1974, he set up the Centre for Overseas Population Studies. This research centre developed into an important centre of demographic research, later dropping 'Overseas' from its title.

Graduate training in demography was also increasingly directed to supply graduates to work in developing countries. A taught master's programme at the LSE was begun in 1965. Brass was instrumental in creating a master's degree in medical demography at the London School of Hygiene, and a large proportion of senior demographers in the UK today studied under him.

During the 1950s and 1960s, there was also an upsurge in interest in population history and in the interaction between demographic and economic and social change in the past. Some of the methods devised for use in countries with inadequate data proved useful in historical demography. David Glass had always been interested in the historical development of population and the history of population theories and policies, and he continued his research in this area. J. A. Banks's study in historical sociology, *Prosperity and Parenthood* (1954), was supervised by Glass. It built on Senior's ideas and anticipated Richard Easterlin's hypothesis that it is income relative to material aspirations that matters for marriage and fertility decisions. In 1965, Glass and David Eversley edited an influential series of essays entitled *Population in History*. It contained, among other contributions, John Hajnal's classic paper on European marriage patterns. In the same year, Peter Laslett published his reassessment of reproductive and family behaviour in the past, entitled *The World We Have Lost*. He and his Cambridge colleagues founded the Cambridge Group for the History of Population and Social Structure, which became one of the leading centres for the study of historical demography in the world. In addition to numerous important studies in historical demography, the Group is responsible for one of the largest studies (if not *the* largest) in demographic history—a reconstruction of the population history of England. This culminated in the publication in 1981 of Tony Wrigley's and Roger Schofield's classic, *The Population History of England 1541–1871*. This historical study has made important contributions to our understanding of the structure and dynamics of families, their relation to population growth, the interaction between demographic and economic change, and to demographic techniques (e.g. 'back projection').

I have so far neglected the contributions of statisticians in the General Register Office, later (from 1970) the Office of Population Censuses and Surveys (OPCS), to the development of demography in Britain. Because the Office provides vital statistics, population projections, and other data, innovations in data collection, techniques, and processing are important for the development of demography. Grebenik (1991) deals with these contributions in greater detail; I will focus on some of the interactions between academic and official demographers. In 1971, the OPCS began to publish its own journal, *Population Trends*, and it encouraged its own officials to publish their results in signed articles there and elsewhere. Academics could also publish in *Population Trends*. The scope of the commentary by the OPCS staff widened, and the number and variety of its publications was extended. The OPCS was also responsible for initiating the Longitudinal Study, in which a sample of persons born on four different dates of the year are followed forward from the 1971 Census. The sample is augmented by births since 1971 as well as by enumeration in subsequent censuses. Registration data are linked to the sample. This is an important resource for demographic and other social research.

The British Society for Population Studies (BSPS), founded in 1973, is an organization in which British official and academic demographers can exchange ideas. It grew out of a Population Study Group formed by the Royal Society, persuaded by Lord Foley (then President of the Royal Society) to set up the Group. It consisted originally of twenty-five members from a variety of disciplines in the biological and social sciences, and met regularly for the discussion of papers on topics connected with population. It met over a period of about eight years. After Lord Foley's death, the Royal Society withdrew its support, and its members formed the nucleus of the BSPS, which continues its activities today.

I close with a consideration of the development, since the Royal Commission on Population, of the discipline of economics in relation to the subject areas that overlap with the traditional interests of sociologists and demographers. Outside Britain, economists have been analysing the family since the early 1960s, bringing economic reasoning and methods to bear on topics such as marriage, fertility, and divorce. Since the late 1970s, research in this area has also been developing in Britain. Economists, including British economists such as Ken Binmore and Robert Sugden,[3] have also shown increasing interest in studying the evolution of social institutions and in peer group influences on behaviour ('social interaction effects'). In a more traditional vein, British economists have been active in studying the economic implications of demographic change, including the impact of population growth on economic development and the impacts of age structure changes on savings and pensions. Research on the relationship between family background and children's subsequent economic position as adults ('social mobility') and on assortative mating has recently assumed more prominence among economists in Britain.

Compared to the large number of sociologists, economists, and demographers active in demographic research in the USA, British social scientists with population interests are relatively rare. For instance, at the 2004 Population Association of America annual meeting, there were thirteen invited sessions and 159 regular sessions, attracting well over 1,000 participants, including many sociologists and economists. Nevertheless, we have seen that British

---

[3] K. Binmore, *Game Theory and the Social Contract: Playing Fair* (Cambridge, MA: MIT Press, 1993); K. Binmore, *Game Theory and the Social Contract: Just Playing* (Cambridge, MA: MIT Press, 1998); R. Sugden, *The Economics of Rights, Co-operation and Welfare* (Oxford: Basil Blackwell, 1986).

demographers have made disproportionate contributions to the development of the subject in relation to their numbers. The British Academy has or had many of the major players in the development of demography in Britain among its Fellows: William Brass, David Glass (also FRS), John Hajnal, Peter Laslett, Roger Schofield, and Tony Wrigley. Britain continues to have demographers of high international standing. At present, there are a dozen BA Fellows elected on the basis of their contributions to population research. While small scale in terms of numbers involved, British demographic research is in good health.

The View from Abroad

8.
A View from a French Sociologist

DOMINIQUE SCHNAPPER

The French are not familiar with British sociology. I will try to illustrate and explain this. I'll refer to a number of factors.

Translations

As a first indicator, British sociology is hardly ever translated into French. An exhaustive examination of the National Library's catalogue confirmed my first impression. What do we find in this catalogue? Dahrendorf's book on the British working class in 1953 was published without much clamour two years later. A volume retracing the work of Goldthorpe and his team was published in a shortened version as *L'ouvrier de l'abondance* by Seuil in 1972. In the years following its publication, it was subsequently cited and discussed by all specialists researching the working class. Richard Hoggart's *The Uses of Literacy* came out in 1970, under the title of *La Culture du Pauvre*, as part of a book series edited by Pierre Bourdieu and published by Minuit, thirteen years after its publication by Chatto & Windus in 1957. This book made a big impact because of its connection to Bourdieu's critique of the 1960s and 1970s. As a result, Hoggart's autobiography was translated in 1991, and co-published by Seuil and Gallimard under the title of *33 Newport Street: Autobiographie d'un intellectuel issu des classes populaires*, three years after its 1988 publication in English by Chatto & Windus.

Let's turn to the current glory of British sociology, Anthony Giddens, who is in Great Britain the most cited and the most widely read British sociologist, along with Marx, Weber, Durkheim, and Parsons and, among the younger generations, before Marx and the others, according to all the tables in Halsey's book. Yet only three of Giddens's books have been translated into

French. The first of them, *The Constitution of Society*, appeared in 1987, three years after its publication by Polity (1984) and it was the only one to be published by a prestigious academic book series, 'Sociologies', edited by Raymond Boudon for Presses Universitaires de France. The second book, *The Consequences of Modernity*, was published in 1994, four years following its English publication (1990), but with the modest humanities publisher, L'Harmattan—a publisher even young doctors, looking to publish their thesis manuscript, are wary of. The third book, *The Third Way*, was published by Seuil in 2002, once again three years after its initial publication (1999), but as part of a non-academic book series. It appeared to be an essentially political publication as suggested by its preface written, not by a sociologist, but by the advocate of social democracy and minority voice in the Blair-weary French Socialist Party, Jacques Delors. As far as I know, no 1950s authors are published in French, with the exception of Dahrendorf's book of 1953.

Gellner, who in France would be regarded as a sociologist, had two of his ethnographies of the Maghreb translated into French in 1981. *Nations and Nationalism* was published by Payot in 1989, six years after its English publication. His study of the psychoanalytical movement came out in 1990, five years after its initial publication and appeared in the 'Sociologies' series edited for Presses Universitaires de France by Raymond Boudon.

The only English-language author, who is really well known, whose work is almost entirely translated into French, who is admired and whose ideas are part of French intellectual debates, is an author, who, despite making his career in England, was educated in Germany. I am of course referring to Norbert Elias. But is he really considered to be a sociologist? We should point out that Mannheim's book on generations was translated only in 1990. Like Elias, Mannheim became a British sociologist late in his life, but he remained relatively marginal in British sociology.

In short, British sociology is not well known and is rather uninfluential in France. On the one hand, its so-called 'classical' form, used by those who Halsey calls the 1950 generation, appears to many to be too rigorous and too marked by that most shameful of things, 'positivism'. This type of sociology is therefore the object of criticism both on the continent and among young British sociologists. On the other hand, the recent radical critique in British sociology emerged later than in France (as far as Marxism is concerned) and later than in the USA (as far as ethnomethodology and postmodernism are concerned). It also sits uncomfortably in the French intellectual landscape (especially in the field of 'race relations' or feminism).

I could use the example of my own experience. Before reading Halsey's book, I of course knew the work of Goldthorpe and Giddens. I had read the social anthropologists. Do I dare to admit that I didn't know Hobhouse? That I only knew Marshall because of his famous seminar on citizenship? That I was familiar with the name Ginsberg only because Shils always claimed that he had two enemies, two Gs, Ginsberg at the LSE and Gurvitch at the Sorbonne?

I had also read the British corpus of literature on race relations and racism on the one hand and the literature dealing with nations and nationalisms from Kedourie and Gellner to Anthony Smith on the other, because this was my research specialism and because I wrote a chapter about the British approach to these questions in *La Relation à l'Autre* (which Robert Miles had accepted to re-read). In my particular field, one cannot ignore British sociology. What has always struck me when reading British sociology is that British research has often been more rigorous than French research because it is based on fieldwork of an anthropological nature, an approach which French scholars have often been reticent about. But this rigourous and serious approach does not make the research less ideological. British researchers are even more scathing, when it comes to criticism of their own nation, than their French counterparts. Finally, we don't have a scholar of the same stature as Michael Banton and sociologists with migrant backgrounds (such as Gilroy or Parekh) do not have equivalent counterparts in France.

Why This Ignorance?

The first reason is obvious. British sociology does not have any of the 'founding fathers' who institutionalized the discipline. There are no Britons among the 'turn of the century generation', to borrow Raymond Aron's phrase, i.e. Weber, Durkheim, or Pareto. English speakers had to read these continental authors, often through translation. Many English-speaking sociologists came to know Weber's work through the interpretations of Parsons and Shils or Gerth and Mills. Those on the continent did not feel the same obligation regarding British sociology, because it developed later than on the continent, where it first became a university discipline.

After the Second World War, despite their 'special relationship' with the USA, the British were late in adopting some of American sociology's advances. Following the disruption to Durkheimian sociology, caused by two world wars, the French went to the USA to study sociology in the 1950s, rather than Britain. The wealth of the universities and the generosity of the scholarships were not the only reasons for this transatlantic migration. British sociology did not stand out clearly enough and appeared, to the French, to be dependent on American sociology anyway. They felt the same way as Wolf Lepenies: 'English (British?) Sociology always remained curiously pallid and lacking in distinct identity.'

Being behind the times in relation to the continent and the USA does not explain everything. British sociology was for a long time closely tied to public policy. It followed in the path of the big social surveys of the nineteenth century and the desire of humanists and other public figures, inspired by the socialist movement, to fight against poverty and improve the lot of the poorer classes. After the Second World War, British sociology accompanied and informed the progressive institutionalization of the welfare state and Labour's policies in the attempt to build a socialist and free society. Until 1968 in any case, it was very largely part of a left-wing but reformist tradition, due to the desire to link social critique and social reform. If it is true that the LSE was, after the War, a sort of Labour think-tank, and if its Director, Anthony Giddens, is generally thought of as one of the major influences on Tony Blair's policies, the opposition with French sociology becomes obvious. French sociologists have never wanted to be associated with a political party which is active in the parliamentary life in what is argued to be a 'bourgeois' society. French sociologists, whose intellectual environment has, for a long time, been dominated by Marxist thinking, and who, today, still claim to be politically radical, elaborate grand theoretical ambitions. They are not interested in sociologists who, through their rational knowledge of social reality, want to contribute to an egalitarian or socialist society, all the while maintaining the political institutions of a liberal society.

110

After the 1970s, many young British sociologists discovered or rediscovered Marxism but, because Marxism had dominated the French intellectual scene for decades and had started to be reinterpreted and refined, this development in Britain couldn't attract the attention nor interest of the French. The British also rediscovered ethnomethodology, but those French researchers who shared the same interest referred directly to American authors rather than passing via the British Isles. French feminists, whose universalist position remains prominent, were also rather reticent about British feminists. As regards the French 'radical' feminists, who remained a minority, their main references were American as well. In addition, the refusal to acknowledge the notion of ethnicity, which characterizes the French sociological tradition in the field of inter-ethnic/race relations, has limited exchanges between French and British specialists working in the areas of ethnic relations and racism.

It therefore seems to French sociologists that the main currents of radical criticism identified by Halsey—Marxism, ethnomethodology, and critiques of race and gender—were taken up by the British only *after* their continental neighbours (as far as Marxism is concerned) and *after* their American counterparts as far as the other schools of thought are concerned. We should also add postmodernism to Halsey's analysis, since this was developed by certain British sociologists. But here, too, a sense of British reticence regarding postmodernism, which had emerged from American colleges and universities, often influenced by French thought, explains why French sociologists did not look for their models or to disseminate their ideas on this side of the Channel, but rather looked to those American colleges and universities instead. In terms of the critique content, British sociologists have, in the last few decades, been less original than they have been in terms of the dissemination of critique. The delay regarding the uptake of these ideas in Britain surely explains why they are not articulated with the critiques of French sociology. Eurostar does not do enough to reinforce intellectual exchange between our two countries.

One should also add a word about the 'parochialism' which reigns to a certain extent on both sides of the Channel. French sociologists are first and foremost interested in French sociology (and afterwards in American sociology). British sociologists are essentially interested in British sociology (and afterwards in American sociology).

The Institutionalization of the Discipline and the Professionalization of Sociologists

In the *History of British Sociology*, Halsey describes the institutionalization of the discipline in universities, in spite of the reluctance shown by more traditional academics at Oxbridge. He also documents the concomitant professionalization of sociologists.

What is striking when one considers these two developments is the parallel historical development in France and Britain, at least from the end of the Second World War. Up until the 1950s, the history was different because of the role played by Durkheim and the Durkheimians who saw themselves not as Labour's think-tank but as the think-tank of the French Republic, which they all believed was still under threat from its enemies. However, even throughout this first period, the first chairs in sociology were created at the same time in both countries. Durkheim introduced the first sociology classes into a French university when he was appointed first as tutor (in 1887), then as professor (in 1898) of pedagogy and social science at the Faculty of Arts at the University of Bordeaux. He became chair of pedagogy at the Sorbonne in 1906 (after having been appointed as a replacement in 1902), a post which was then changed into 'the Sorbonne chair of sociology' in 1912. The first chair of sociology in Britain was created in 1907.

The discipline remained equally marginal in both countries until the aftermath of the Second World War, when it developed enormously during the 1960 and 1970s, in parallel with the democratization of liberal societies.

It was less the result of direct action taken by the 1950 generation, described by Halsey, which explains this development than the more generalized growth and normalization of sociology as a discipline through the opening up of universities. Sociology is the daughter of democracy. Sociology developed enormously in France throughout the 1960s and 1970s. On this side of the Channel, the development of sociology owed a lot to the Robbins Report of 1963 and, after the 1980s Thatcher crisis years, to the integration of polytechnics into the university system in 1992. Today, 2,000 university teachers teach sociology to 24,000 students in Britain, according to Halsey. It is estimated that 1,200 French university teachers (including the CNRS corps of researchers) teach some 12,000 students in France. Sociology, which is about critical reasoning vis-à-vis society, is inextricably linked to the democratization of education and to democracy itself.

The make-up and the features of the corps of sociologists are very similar in both countries. In France, the first generation of sociologists often came from a philosophy background. In Britain, they came from social work backgrounds, the empirical disciplines of the big surveys of the nineteenth century, and even from literature. On both sides of the Channel, we find a concentration of marginalized individuals: foreigners, Jews, people who had broken away from their social milieu or from their academic fields, journalists. These characteristics also hold true for the founders of the Chicago School. According to Halsey, in Britain, one-third of those sociologists born before 1930 were immigrants. The high proportion of Jewish sociologists is striking in France; they were over-represented among the Durkheimians, as they were in the following generation with Gurvitch, who was born in Russia in 1894, Friedman who was born in France in 1904 of immigrant parents, and Aron, who was born in 1905 into an old Jewish French family linked to the Durkheim family. Simple sociological analysis suggests that those who are marginal in society become marginal intellectuals—and this was certainly the case for sociology, which was regarded with disdain by the advocates of classical culture. Such analysis also shows that 'marginals' are more likely to question the social order, which for them is not self-evident. We should also take into account that the first generations of sociologists, who were the most 'marginal', had a wide range of philosophical and historical reference; they also spoke and were familiar with foreign languages and cultures. Professionalization had an intellectual cost.

From the 1960s onwards, the sociology population became more mainstream as it grew larger, even if it remained smaller than the other university disciplines. Sociologists of the post-1960 generation are no longer individuals on the margins of society. Like other students, they are middle class and less often from working-class backgrounds. They have professionalized. They have studied the 'classics' in accordance with a university programme of study and they master the essential statistical packages and methods. On the other hand, they do not have the same philosophy background and they don't know foreign languages. Now, a British sociologist usually quotes *Le Suicide*, by referring to the most commonly used translation, published in 1957, as opposed to referring to the date when the book was first published in French (1897).

Sociologists were at the centre of the events of 1968 in both countries. This gave them an ambiguous image in France, to use an understatement, and, more often than not, a negative image in Britain. Today, the discipline whose image was inflated in the 1948–68 period, then vilified from the 1970s onwards with the active participation of sociologists in the 1968 events, is questioning itself about its future. Is there still a place for reflection based on rational and critical social enquiry without, on the other hand, giving into the passions of radical denunciation?

The Problem of Boundaries

This self-questioning is not new. The problem of boundaries is perhaps even constitutive of sociology itself. Everything depends on how we define sociology; that is, how we reconcile a specific intellectual standpoint—already articulated by Montesquieu and Tocqueville and even the openly normative stance of classical philosophy—with the institutionalization of a new academic discipline. As Halsey puts it: 'Sociology has no agreed boundaries and birthday. It is probably coincident with civilization. Its boundaries are shifting and disputed.' And it seems to me to be a little too pragmatic, as only an Englishman even of German origin can be, to say, like Dahrendorf did, that 'Sociology is what the LSE does or did', or a little too radical to say that sociology exists only when it develops analysis based on statistical data.

Sociology is defined by its perpetual search for its own definition. For a long time, the British definition of sociology was a lot more modest and narrow than the French definition. This was because the British sociologists were faced with a prestigious discipline linked to imperial ambitions, social anthropology. Malinowski, Radcliffe-Brown, Evans-Pritchard, Fortes, Firth, and Leach have won a worldwide reputation. Sociology was also in contest with literature and literary criticism. Charles Dickens, like Balzac, was regarded by his critics, the most famous of whom was Leavis, as one of the true sociologists. Social criticism of Victorian capitalism was carried out by writers, as illustrated by Raymond

Willams's book, *Culture and Society*, and later by the work of Lepenies on the three cultures. Social criticism was not part of the wider project of studying society as it was defined on the continent. According to Perry Anderson, the Marxist thinker and radical critic of British sociology, the British did not need to construct a veritable sociology in opposition to socialism and Marxism, since the influence of these ideas on the British Isles was not strong enough to compel them to do so.

The sociology that Durkheim wanted to develop was more ambitious and included anthropological enquiry. The French sociologists of the former generations have read the British social anthropologists. In other words, research on society as a whole was carried out by sociologists in France and social anthropologists in Britain. Social anthropology was only founded in France after the Second World War, under the influence of Lévi-Strauss, who, having spent the war years in New York, learnt a lot about anglophone social anthropology. On the other hand, certain aspects of British sociology resemble the statistical work carried out by large public institutions in France, such as the Institut d'Études Démographiques (INED) or the Institut National de Statistiques et D'Études Économiques (INSEE). Cultural studies would be an integral part of French sociology while public policy studies remain somewhat marginal. When Halsey describes the institutionalization of the discipline, he only evokes in passing social anthropologists from Malinowski to Gellner or cultural studies authors; he does not cite political scientists, such as Ralph Miliband, who would be regarded as sociologists in France.

However, at the same time, French sociology has lost some of its specificity by becoming part of a wider social sciences project, whereas British sociology has put forward its viewpoint more clearly by concentrating on problems of social structure. This explains the influence of British sociology on a number of European countries, especially those in northern Europe. In contrast, the French are conspicuously absent in all sorts of international organizations of sociology.

Up until 1968, British sociology appeared to be focused on a rigorous and rather narrow understanding of the discipline: empirical studies of the anthropological and statistical type of class structures, mobility, the working class, education, the family, industrial structures, race relations in urban spaces. These studies were its strength. In doing this, the British adopted a definition of their discipline in contrast to the French, who more ambitiously refused any strict demarcation of their field. But by being more interdisciplinary and concerned about methodological critique, French sociologists also run the risk of becoming 'essayists' as a result of their somewhat excessive ambitions to not bow down to the strict rules of research. This in turn limits the French contribution to knowledge. On the other hand, I can also see a danger in the excessive specialization of British sociologists, which leads them to create more and more specialized journals. This danger links sociology too closely to social practices and, as a result, the intellectual exercise of understanding society might be limited.

The Strengths of British Sociology

Being myself an adept follower of so-called classical sociology—which I understand as a project to understand social realities by overcoming the opposition between qualitative and quantitative methods in order to arrive at the most objective understanding as possible—my viewpoint will inevitably be influenced by this personal conception. Since, generally, the problem of sociology is linked to its definition and its boundaries, my interpretation cannot be independent of my own understanding of sociology.

The first strength of British sociology lies in the organization of the profession. The debates and critiques are sharp and sometimes heated. *You* have a conflict, where mutual disdain is affirmed, between the two Gs—that is, Goldthorpe and Giddens. *We* have a similar conflict between two Bs—that is, Bourdieu and Boudon. In both countries, there are warring factions. Naturally, we are sociologist enough to realize that such conflicts can be found across all intellectual disciplines. But what is specific about sociology is that the accusations are not restricted to the quality of the sociology, but extend to the quality of the sociologist. 'He/she is not a real sociologist' is the common criticism, since we are in a field which is unsure of its own definition. This explains the lack of direct intellectual exchange. And yet the strength of a discipline stems from the intellectual debates it stimulates. The organization of the field in Britain balances some of these limitations, at least to a much greater extent than in France. Having been President of the French

116

Sociological Society, I can be affirmative; it certainly is not a mirror or a motor of sociological research.

But the main strength of British sociology seems to me to be the quantity and quality of empirical research on those important social problems which I've already mentioned: social classes, mobility, poverty, exclusion, sociology of education, urban race relations. All these issues are approached in the best of anthropological and statistical traditions and therefore bring concrete knowledge about the salient social problems of contemporary society. In this sense, one can't help observing that the so-called classical sociologists—mainly the 1950s generation and those who carry out similar research—hostile or indifferent as they are to Marxism, are less likely to engage in the recent currents of radical critique than their French counterparts.

There are two groups in Britain which don't have an equivalent in France. The first concerns those conservative academics, who have remained fundamentally critical to the social sciences, and who admitted sociology as a discipline to Oxbridge only with great reluctance and because they were forced to. The second group concerns the so-called classical sociologists, represented by the 1950s generation and its students. This group maintains an intellectual tradition based on rigorous empirical research, whether it is statistical or anthropological.

If recent currents of critical sociology don't seem to me to be all that remarkable, this is not only because I am personally reticent about them. It is also because these currents don't seem to be original or distinct from the development of critical sociology in other countries. The most recent debates—postmodernism, multiculturalism, critiques of racism, feminism—are part of wider currents of sociology which are not specific to Britain and which depend heavily on American sociology. But perhaps—and lets be optimistic about this—this trend is the sign that sociology is a universal intellectual discipline and it is not surprising that, today, national specificities are progressively on the wane. Does a 'national sociology' still exist? After all, and let's be 'classical' until the end, truth is one and indivisible.

I'd like to finish with an anecdote, the personal nature of which I hope you will excuse. In 1944, Lionel Robbins wanted Raymond Aron, who had become his friend during the war years in London, to become the chair of sociology at the LSE. But my father dreamed of coming back to France and he refused to apply for the post. If he had agreed to Lionel Robbins's suggestion and if he had been selected, I am too much of a sociologist to think that the history of British sociology would have been transformed. But I can't help thinking today that, if he had accepted this proposition, I would probably be among you, as a British sociologist, listening to another French sociologist giving the French point of view on British sociology. That's the way life goes.

Note: I would like to thank Nadia Kiwan for translating this essay.

9.
A View from Sweden

ROBERT ERIKSON

To write about a subject one knows less about than the audience is somewhat of a kamikaze project—it may easily end in a big crash. Being thus situated I will start by discussing sociology in general, in this way trying to even out the differences in acquaintance with the subject-matter, and partly base my views of British sociology on comparisons with the Swedish situation.

The rationale behind discussing sociology in general in a volume devoted to British sociology is my impression that British sociology is not all that much different from sociology in most other countries; so, by writing about sociology in general, I hope to say something about sociology in Britain.

A Divided Discipline

It seems quite clear to me that if by sociology we mean what is taught and studied at sociology departments around the world, sociology is a divided discipline. I am certain that if sociology students at one Swedish university were to sit an exam given to sociology students at any other university—in Sweden or elsewhere—they would do much worse than would be the case for students in other social sciences, say economics. I leave it to you to consider whether this would also be true within Britain or whether the system of external examiners at the universities on the British Isles makes curricula and teaching more similar here than elsewhere among universities.

Thus, various forms of intellectual activity run under the name of sociology. This is certainly not a new phenomenon, C. Wright Mills (1959) characterized sociological practice at Harvard and Columbia in the 1950s as Grand Theory and Abstracted Empiricism, respectively. My impression, though, is that the division has become deeper. That is, to stick to my operational definition, I believe that sociology students some fifty years ago would have done better in the exams of other departments than would be the case today. This is partly due to varying effects of prevailing ideologies, that is the, now perhaps fading, influence of Marxism and the strong influence of feminism present in some departments but not in others.

Even more important for the split may be where sociology teachers find the essence of the subject—middle range theories, globalization, and world system theories or cultural studies—and if they find quantitative or qualitative methods as the one and only way to find out about the social world. The 'cultural turn' seems to have had a profound influence on some practitioners of the subject, and social constructivism seems in some circles to be the appropriate standpoint on the philosophy of science.

Protagonists of the different varieties of sociology claim, with more or less success, the supremacy of their own preferred form. However, an overall dialogue seems to be lacking. My experience is that if we, mostly by mistake, at a conference have to listen to the supporter of some other 'sociology' than our own, we stay absent-minded and then return to our 'own' work groups; and I don't think that I differ from most other sociologists in finding some of the other forms of sociology rather questionable. In my case, I have great difficulty in accepting some varieties in which great statements are made without a sign of empirical support, and sometimes without even the possibility of finding such support; and likewise in accepting the understanding of 'social theory' as an explication of concepts and elaborations of taxonomies, which by definition are neither true nor false.

A problem for sociology, and for most of the other social sciences, is that it has a partly non-scientific background; approaches and hypotheses may be chosen on grounds of value positions. This is fully acceptable on condition that arguments are scrutinized on the basis of their internal consistency and empirical validity, and that researchers put more effort in checking results, which are in line with their ideological position than those that go against it. Sometimes, however, I get the impression that the conclusion was there first and the arguments found afterwards. The theoretical split under all circumstances becomes more difficult to overcome if it is supported by ideological positions.

Pressly claimed that new interpretations of historical events appear more because of ideological commitments and personal experiences of new generations of researchers than because earlier interpretations and theories are falsified by empirical results (Pressly 1954, cited by Rule 1988). Theoretical 'progress' in history appears, according to Pressly, as a succession of interpretations of events where new ones follow older ones without the latter being eliminated by empirical observations. Is it not also true for sociology that each generation writes its own sociology? The remarkable change in the orientation of sociology around 1970 was hardly the result of new theoretical insights or new empirical results, and, again, the inflow of feminist thinking during the last decades did not appear because of such reasons.

Some sociologists regard their intellectual activity as a vehicle for social change rather than as work within an academic discipline. Again, I cannot find this problematic on condition that, in their academic work, they stick to the rules of science; they use empirical evidence to test their hypotheses rather than to illustrate them; and they publish results that are in contradiction to their aims. There is, given a strong commitment to a particular cause, a risk of accepting only the 'right' conclusions and of assuming that the theory is true, so empirical observations are needed only to illustrate it. The risk seems to be there regardless of the researcher's ideological position, and we all need to make serious efforts to avoid it.

It may be natural that the social sciences are influenced by the societal development and waves of varying ideological commitment, but it means that our theories and models are more conditional than we perhaps want to admit. It means that we in sociology have many theoretical positions, which their upholders have chosen not because of theoretical consistency and empirical support but because they are in accordance with the researchers' experience and ideological position, or perhaps just because they are *en vogue*.

We find in too many areas of sociology theories and hypotheses, whose internal consistency is unclear and, especially, whose empirical testability is uncertain and sometimes non-existent. I would expect that such theories will in the long run be forgotten, not because they are falsified by empirical observations, but because they will go out of fashion.

Some practitioners keep with the old fashions while others quickly move on to new ones and the elimination of theories through empirical falsification only works in the long run—if accepted at all—so in the short run we have a discipline in which we may agree on the central object of study, but in which there is no common and accepted theory. We rather have several theories, fragments of theories, and empirical generalizations, which may or may not be compatible. My impression is that British sociology in all these respects is no different from sociology in other parts of the world.

But even if there are divisions in sociology in Britain, the distribution of the various factions seems to differ from what is the case in many other countries. For this occasion I have gone through the British sociology journals. My immediate impression was that very few articles were based on a quantitative analysis and even fewer on more advanced quantitative techniques. Before trying to systematize this impression I came to the first issue of *Sociology* for 2004 and found that Payne, Williams, and Chamberlain (2004) had already done the necessary job. They show that the number of papers about quantitative sociology in the general sociology journals (*British Journal of Sociology*, *Sociology*, and *Sociological Review*) from 1999 and 2000 is surprisingly low; only around one paper in ten includes bivariate or multivariate analyses. Only the more specialized *Work, Employment and Society* contains a substantial number of quantitative sociology papers; around one-third of the total number in this journal include multivariate analysis. But this seems not to be the whole story. I counted the number of articles on quantitative sociology with non-British authors in the same two volumes of the *British Journal of Sociology* and *Sociology*. (I did not bother to check *Sociological Review* since, according to Payne, Williams, and Chamberlain, it contains no papers using multivariate techniques.) Of fourteen papers with multivariate analysis of some kind in the *British Journal of Sociology*, six were written by authors outside the UK; and of eight in *Sociology*, only four were written by British authors.[1] Thus of 244 articles in the mainstream journals, ten written by British authors include multivariate analyses.

---

[1] I seem to have missed one article, which Payne, Williams, and Chamberlain classified as using multivariate analysis, but the overall impression is clearly correct.

Ten out of 244 is a remarkably small proportion even if several of the non-quantitative papers also have non-British authors. A look in the *American Sociological Review* or the *American Journal of Sociology* shows a completely different picture, perhaps the mirror image. But quantitatively based analyses are common in Europe as well. Far more than half of the articles in the *European Sociological Review* are based on quantitative multivariate approaches. In the 1999 volume of *Revue Française de Sociologie*, six out of twenty-two articles include multivariate analyses and more than half the papers in the 1999 volumes of *Kölner Zeitschrift für Soziologie und Sozialpsychologie* and *Zeitschrift für Soziologie* are based on various forms of such analyses. Without having checked I believe that the importance of quantitative research is greater also in the Netherlands and Sweden than in Britain, as it seems from looking at the mainstream British journals. Thus Dutch, Swedish, and, in fact, British sociologists are among the most common authors of papers in the *European Sociological Review*, where, as mentioned, the vast majority of the papers are based on quantitative techniques. Methodological approaches which are common or even standard in other countries seem to be rare in British sociology, at least as judged from the British journals. Payne, Williams, and Chamberlain conclude that there is a need for more quantitative analysis in sociology in Britain.

However, that part of the study by Payne, Williams, and Chamberlain regarding *Work, Employment and Society*, and the relatively large number of British authors in the *European Sociological Review* show that the situation in British sociology is not so one-sided as the distribution of articles in the general journals indicates and my personal experience of reading papers by British sociologists likewise suggests that much quantitative work is done here, while the relative amount of such work may have decreased in recent years. The initiative by the ESRC in favour of building capacity for quantitative work does not seem to have had much impact yet. Furthermore, my impression is that most of the quantitative work is done at research institutes, like the Cathy Marsh Centre in Manchester or the Institute for Social and Economic Research at the University of Essex, rather than in university departments. Perhaps I could propose that Britain has institutes for sociological research and departments of cultural studies.

Payne, Williams, and Chamberlain suggest that the large proportion of qualitative research in the British journals is not due to quantitatively oriented British sociologists publishing their papers outside Britain, but to the fact that nearly all British sociologists use qualitative approaches. Even if this is the case, some of the best quantitative sociology in the world is produced in this country by authors such as Richard Breen, Duncan Gallie, John Goldthorpe, Anthony Heath, and Gordon Marshall; all members of the British Academy. Since they have mostly published their articles in international journals—even if papers by them have appeared in the *British Journal of Sociology*, *Sociology*, and *Work, Employment and Society*—it must be that the extreme predominance of the qualitative approach in the mainstream British journals is due to some extent to the choice of forum by British authors of a quantitative inclination.

Literature or Science?

In his book on British sociology, Halsey (2004) takes up an issue which is related, but certainly not identical, to the one on using quantitative or qualitative methodological approaches. Halsey's first chapter reviews the early debate on whether sociology should be regarded as literature or science or, to put it otherwise, whether most insight into societal processes will be produced by literary accounts or through systematic description and analysis. I am unclear whether Halsey finds that the 'battle' is won by the scientific side or not, but I certainly do not think this to be the case. Still in 1988 Wolf Lepenies placed sociology in between literature and science, but he seemed to take the view that it was better if it leaned towards literature rather than in the other direction. Let me use an example from Scandinavia to make clear why I have doubts about whether sociologists generally look at sociology as a social science.

Around fifteen years ago I conducted a survey of how Swedish and Norwegian sociologists looked at their discipline. Among other questions, I asked which book or article the respondents regarded as most important among those published in the last ten years. In each country one author was mentioned much more often than any other: in Norway, Dag Österberg by 25 per cent of those answering; in Sweden, Johan Asplund by around 17 per cent. Both authors are regarded as theorists, Asplund especially as an expert on social psychology.

However, when I asked in which areas of sociology the most important contributions had been made by Norwegian and Swedish sociologists, respectively, neither theory nor social psychology was mentioned more than occasionally. How can this anomaly be understood?

Österberg and Asplund are both good authors whose works are a pleasure to read. It may then be that the literary qualities of their work and their noted positions in cultural circles in Scandinavia made many of their colleagues regard them as the foremost sociologists of our countries. This could mean that for many sociologists it is not the systematic understanding of societal conditions and processes but the elegant formulation and the stimulating narrative that make a sociological work important. The sociological ideal may for many sociologists be artistic rather than scientific; to publish an article in one of the major cultural journals may then be regarded as a greater merit than to publish a paper in a sociological journal.

However, no sociologist can match the foremost authors in giving an image of the passions and problems of human interaction, so it seems as if an artistic ideal for sociology would make the great authors the leading sociologists. A literary work seems true because the author describes what we have felt and experienced, by giving an account of a social world, of interpersonal conflicts, of individual passions that we find to be true. But the literary work does not convince the person to whom it does not speak. It is on this point that systematic social science has its strength. It provides the evidence for a specific way of understanding a social process, evidence that can be checked by the disbeliever. A better understanding of a phenomenon can be found thanks to the possibility of one scientist building on the work of other scientists, a cumulation of knowledge that is not possible within literature.

Readers of a sociological account of some societal phenomenon should be able to discern the logical coherence of the arguments, to check whether the empirical observations relate to the arguments, and to decide if the conclusions follow. Thereby, they will be able to judge whether they find the account dependable and, if not, be able to spell out why this is the case. However, if they are to convince others that they are right in not finding the evidence conclusive, they must be able to show where the account of the phenomenon does not hold.

My conclusion is that it is a problem for sociology if sociologists still believe that literature rather than science is the appropriate way of increasing our knowledge about society and societal processes. It could be added that it is a further problem if they then resort to the practice of writing books out of books, regardless of the literary value of what they produce.

The British Sociological Association—Professional Organization or Learned Society?

Throughout Jennifer Platt's (2003) book on the BSA runs the question of whether it should be regarded as a professional organization or a learned society. This seems to be an appropriate issue to raise at the conference co-organized by the British Academy and the BSA.

When preparing this paper, actually before I had the chance to read Platt's book, I tried to find out about the relation between the Academy and the BSA. To my surprise I found no member of the Academy on any committee of the Association. To find out whether this was typical for Britain, I looked at the Council of the Royal Economic Society. It turns out to hold several highly distinguished fellows of the Academy. Platt lists the members of the BSA executive committee from the start in 1951. I could then search backwards for Academy fellows and I had to go back to 1968–9 before David Lockwood's name appeared, although at that time he, of course, had not yet been elected to the Academy. I might have missed a name or two, but it seems clear that the logical intersection of membership of the Academy and the BSA Council is empty or close to empty. Why this is the case is obviously open to varying interpretations. This is all the more so since members of the Sociology section of the Academy are not generally withdrawing from organizational work; many of them are active in international organizations like the International Sociological Association (ISA), the European Consortium for Sociological Research (ECSR), and EU networks.

That none of the most distinguished sociologists in Britain is involved in the affairs of the BSA and that this has been the case for several decades suggests, at least to me, that the Association, unlike the Royal Economic Society, cannot be regarded as a national learned society, for I believe that such an organization should engage the leading members of the discipline.

The BSA could anyway claim that it has an important characteristic of a learned society since it takes responsibility for sociology as science in publishing two journals, *Sociology* and *Work, Employment and Society*. My impression is that while papers in the latter often are of reasonable quality, *Sociology* has in recent years, on the whole, not been worth following. If this is correct—or I should perhaps say if many other sociologists share my view—this is all the more important for the reputation of the Association, since *Sociology* is its mainstream journal. It is here that the BSA can show that it takes responsibility for the quality of all of sociology in Britain. Prejudices should not just be accepted, so to check mine I read all the articles in the then latest issue of *Sociology* (vol. 38, 1, February 2004).

I am afraid that the reading supported my initial impression. Two papers raise questions, which for good reasons were taken up in the journal of a professional organization, since they are issues which are relevant for the profession. The first is that by Payne, Williams, and Chamberlain, on the characteristics of publications by British sociologists. The second is by Parry and Mauthner on the issue of archiving qualitative data: I do not agree with their conclusion, but the issue is obviously important to a professional society of sociologists. But the other full-scale papers were overall disappointing to this reader.

The paper that I found most interesting is essentially based on an interview with one person; the aim is to develop a sociology of shyness. It is well known that Freud, with scientific ambitions, developed psychoanalysis on the basis of single cases, but I don't think that it is wise to follow his example. The author of the paper on shyness, Susie Scott, uses Mead's distinction between the I and the me, which gives her a useful frame for her discussion. It is then surprising that she seems to leave the definition of shyness to the interviewee, giving the reader difficulties in knowing exactly what should be explained; furthermore she does not try to check to what extent her theoretical outline gives any insight to the situation of her other fifteen interviewees, making the reader wonder how generalizable her ideas are.

Another paper seeks to give us insight into perceptions of inequality on the basis of a 'non-random theoretical sample' of twenty-eight women, where, however, no theoretical principles of sampling are provided. Those interviewed are classified into three groups: those who endorse the present situation, those who oppose it, and those who accommodate to it. I cannot see that more information is provided than that there are women who hold each of these three positions.

In one paper it is suggested, with reference to Bourdieu, that women architects are not promoted because male architects partly take on female roles while simultaneously exerting masculine domination and, furthermore, that female architects find it difficult to combine work and parenting.

From one of the papers the reader gets interesting insights into the problems that health professionals face when giving information to pregnant women. Then, to the reader's surprise, it ends with a reference to Scambler (2001) in a plea 'for moving beyond positivist research that aims to predict health inequalities by studying variables' since, it seems, health inequalities may be understood as indirect and largely unintended 'consequences of the behaviours of members of the power elite informed by the capitalist executive', and furthermore that 'among numerous mechanisms the elite control the means of production and profit and, as the system, they colonize the life world, by absorbing it into the political/economic system, and turning social issues into technical ones'.

One paper argues that, in discussing problems related to the use of alcohol and drugs, authorities do not emphasize the pleasure following from drinking; another paper is an argument for giving children more to say in politics. These papers may be enjoyable to read, but they hardly merit space in a professional journal.

My problem with these papers is not that they are based on qualitative methods—even if I am firmly placed on the quantitative side—but that, overall, they do not stick to what I regard as an accepted logic of inference. On this point I find the positions of King, Keohane, and Verba (1994) and Goldthorpe (2000) apt. That is, the logic of scientific inference is in principle no different in qualitative and quantitative research.

I must add that I do not find articles good just because they are

128

based on quantitative analyses. There is a lot of mindless empiricism where problems are chosen, regardless of their substantial interest, because they can be approached through a preferred technique.

The presentation of empirical observations in many of the articles is in the form of a large number of excerpts from interviews made with a few subjects. Thus, a story is told but, as Teune (1997, quoted from Goldthorpe 2000) has pointed out, 'a story is no theory', and little more than the story is told in most of the papers. These stories, like literature, can convince only those to whom they speak, those who happen to interpret the interview in the same way as the authors. I lack rules by which the interviews relate to theoretical conclusions.

Some of the authors do not seem to have bothered to choose interviewees so that variation in important respects is guaranteed in the groups they study. Two of the papers are based on snowball sampling. This is a technique for finding respondents in situations where those who should be studied cannot be identified by other means. But is there really no other way of finding architects or English people in Scotland? The consequence of finding respondents in this way for the study of Englishmen in Scotland was that, if I have understood it correctly, no information on the situation of an English worker was elicited, since the researchers started by interviewing some acquaintances and then friends to these persons, and the segregation of social contacts gave the result that they never reached the working class. One strength of qualitative studies, as I see it, is the possibility of a high degree of variation in crucial respects even in a small sample.

British sociology is in a bad shape if this issue of the journal is representative of the prevailing standards. I am aware that I open myself to my own critique, since I have studied only one issue of the journal. However, having looked in many other issues, I am fully convinced that this one is not very different from most of the others published in the last years. If the BSA wishes to live up to the expectation of being a learned society it will certainly have to put much work into bringing its general sociological journal up to an international standard.

Conclusion

British sociology, like sociology in the rest of the world, is divided into varieties, which differ in both theoretical and methodological approaches. However, qualitative approaches seem much more common here than in other countries. It seems, furthermore, as if a rather unsatisfactory style of qualitative analysis has become common in Britain—a style in which stringent inference is replaced by quotations from interviews and hardly anything else. An essential task for the British Academy and the British Sociological Association is to continue from this common initiative to try to bring the whole of British sociology closer to the international mainstream. Then we in all countries should work together for a better sociology.

Note. Helpful comments on earlier drafts have been given by John H. Goldthorpe, Jan O. Jonsson, Gordon Marshall, and Michael Tåhlin.

References

Goldthorpe, John H. (2000), *On Sociology*, Oxford: Oxford University Press.

Halsey, A. H. (2004), *A History of Sociology in Britain*, Oxford: Oxford University Press.

King, Gary, Keohane, Robert O., and Verba, Sidney (1994), *Designing Social Inquiry: Scientific Inference in Qualitative Research*, Princeton: Princeton University Press.

Lepenies, Wolf (1988), *Between Literature and Science: The Rise of Sociology*, Cambridge: Cambridge University Press.

Mills, C. Wright (1959), *The Sociological Imagination*, New York: Oxford University Press.

Payne, Geoff, Williams, Malcolm, and Chamberlain, Suzanne (2004), 'Methodological Pluralism in British Sociology', *Sociology* 35, pp. 153–63.

Platt, Jennifer (2003), *The British Sociological Association: A Sociological History*, Durham: sociologypress.

Pressly, Thomas, J. (1954), *Americans Interpret Their Civil War*, Princeton: Princeton University Press.

Rule, James B. (1988), *Theories of Civil Violence*, Berkeley: University of California Press.

Scambler, Graham (2001), 'Class, Power and the Durability of Health Inequalities', in G. Scambler (ed.), *Habermas, Critical Theory and Health*, London: Routledge.

Teune, Henry (1997), 'Stories, Observations, Systems, Theories', *Comparative Social Research* 16, pp. 73–83.

10.
A View from Europe

COLIN CROUCH

In the piece I have contributed to Chelly Halsey's book, I draw an analogy which I have often used between the history of sociology and the history of the Habsburg Empire. The Habsburg Empire claimed to be 'the' empire and to have legitimate sovereignty over the whole of Europe. But it did not have a structure capable of resisting the tough, tightly organized nation-states like France, Spain, England, the Netherlands, and eventually—and, for the Habsburgs, fatally—Prussia. So gradually it moved away from the cockpit of nation-states that constituted western Europe towards the eastern and southern margins of the continent. It finally became a discontented jumble of margins. In the same way, Talcott Parsons tried to claim that sociology was the empress of the social sciences; economics, political science, and the others being allocated their places within her realm. But sociology could not match the tougher, tighter theoretical structures of political science, economics, psychology, and even possibly anthropology. It became an internally divided subject, cultivating the margins.

There is, however, another way of modelling the imperial claims of sociology, and that is to see it as a subject that operates at the crossing-points. This is sociology seen not as the Habsburg Empire, but as Belgium. Not a good place to be when boundaries are tightly drawn and tenaciously defended as in 1914 or 1939, but a very useful location when integration is on the agenda. In the natural sciences during the last twenty years or so the most significant developments have taken place at the interstices between disciplines. Molecular biology brings chemists and biologists together, and genetics brings together people from a whole range of scientific disciplines who are rediscovering the nodes where they cross with each other. Indeed, the sociology of science itself tells us that major scientific advances, as opposed to merely incremental ones, are likely to come from research institutes where people are forced to rub shoulders with people from other disciplines over lunch. Or sometimes the innovations come from people whose training and experience have been in one particular area but at a certain point in their lives they become interested in problems presented by a different one with which they have come into contact. So it is time and again in the interstices between one specialist discipline and another that intellectual innovation is to be found.

It is, however, very difficult to make that happen in practice. Natural scientists have found the process difficult, especially at the point of translating research advance into courses and teaching Because of the exponential growth in knowledge, scientific endeavour has become more and more specialized. Matters are therefore moving in two opposed directions at once. On the one hand, innovations are emerging at the interstices; but, on the other, the structure of the courses being taught is becoming more and more rigidly specialized. Those concerned about this are actively involved in reforms intended to restore an interdisciplinary core to the courses they are teaching. But they find it hard, because the more interdisciplinary courses are created that can, inevitably, be no more than introductions, the less anyone ever really learns about anything.

Now this same theme was already present in the very interesting report that John Westergaard wrote about our own discipline of sociology in 1989.[1] In that report, he pointed out in another geopolitical analogy that sociology, after the dismantling of its heartland which had taken place in the preceding years, had become what he called a 'diaspora subject'. Sociologists were being scattered about all over the place. They were to be found teaching engineers, accountants, and medical practitioners for whom sociology was now a part, and in some universities a compulsory part, of their vocational training. This could at first sight be regarded as a triumph for the discipline. But, as Westergaard asked in his report, what happens if that's all there is to it? Who is going to produce the sociologists of the future? A department of engineering that employs sociologists will turn out engineers who have some

---

[1] John Westergaard and Ray Pahl, 'Looking Backwards and Forwards: The UGC's Review of Sociology', *British Journal of Sociology* 40 (1989), pp. 374–92.

understanding of sociological variables, and that is no doubt a good thing. But it will not turn out the next generation of sociologists. As sociology moves into interdisciplinary areas, it faces the same dilemma as the natural sciences which are going the same way. One may be doing very important and original work, but who is looking after the subject back home? As in all diasporas, the homeland starts to disappear altogether, and this is the point which I think sociology is now reaching. We are well placed to play our part in innovative interdisciplinary research linked up with other people. But what is the base from which we are coming? As Robert Erikson shows us in Chapter 9 of this volume, the base often turns out to be of an unhelpful kind when it comes to the sort of interstitial collaboration I have in mind. What is needed, as sociological theory itself would imply, is a discipline that is lightly embedded in other subjects. If it is too deeply embedded, it becomes a discipline populated entirely by specialized nomads. But, if it remains too deeply enmeshed in its own preoccupations, its practitioners find they cannot properly talk to anybody else—which is what is happening to economics.

So what does 'light embeddedness' actually mean? Given that there are at the moment opportunities for interdisciplinary advances across a number of social-scientific fields, our discipline should be well placed to take part. But it isn't as well placed as it ought to be because of the way in which it is currently conducting its own affairs. I believe that we could construct courses for bachelors and masters degrees, and write the necessary textbooks, in a way that would both provide a solid grounding in sociology as such and also make sociology graduates available for interstitial research and engagement with other disciplines. The challenge is to restructure the subject so that, at the same time, it preserves its core but relates that core to other disciplines. The two disciplines which are critical to this, on account of their theoretical approaches as well as their substantive subject-matter, are economics and political science. If we were able to construct a sociology which could sustain constructive dialogues with these and perhaps others of the social sciences also, it would be a sociology very different from what is currently taught in Britain. This may to some extent apply equally to other countries. But I do think that there is a particular British problem here and that to resolve it would require a fundamental change.

As it happens, the kind of training which such a change would call for is very much the kind of training that Chelly Halsey and others of his generation were given by the old BSc Econ degree at the LSE. Sociology in those days was directly linked to history and philosophy as well as to economics and political science. This meant that even when as a sociologist one went on to do research of a more specialized kind, one was still thinking of it as a subject which had those links. In the 1970s those links were torn apart, initially because the economists in particular were no longer prepared to have any interdisciplinary contact with sociology at all. The degree still exists in name. But it no longer has the special character that it used to have; and the economists would claim that it is because our respective disciplinary needs have become so specialized that there just is not time any longer for either of us to poke around in each other's subjects. That, as I have said, is the problem which the natural sciences have also been facing. But, unless we find some means of retaining these links, we are going to lose the capacity for innovation which we need to preserve.

There is, however, a field called neo-institutionalism in which an increasing amount of good research is being done and which is challenging some of the orthodoxies of the neo-classical economics and neo-liberal political science which have come to dominate the intellectual world since the decline of Keynesianism in the 1970s. There is now a serious debate both at the level of theory and in the formulation and execution of programmes of empirical research in which sociologists are taking part. There is even something called sociological neo-institutionalism which is enabling sociologists who share the new approach to hide within a definition that puts them in a select little group to which they can claim to belong. It will be interesting to see what exactly sociological neo-institutionalism turns out to mean. Usually, it seems to involve bringing the analysis of cultural differences and subjective perceptions to bear on the analysis of institutional change. This might seem to suggest that sociologists are just one particular branch of neo-institutionalism. But, it seems to me that if any discipline owns the concept of institutions as such it is sociology. As of now, where neo-institutionalist theses are starting to be written, the chances are that citations as to where the concept of an institution comes from will be about 60 per cent Douglass C. North and 40 per cent Peter Hall—the one an economic historian and the other a political scientist. Both of them are very good at what they do. But their concepts of an institution are in fact less profound and less solidly grounded than the concept of an institution as defined by the sociological tradition. The emerging neo-institutionalist paradigm is one to which sociology can and should be central. But, for that to be possible, we need to ensure that the training we are giving to our undergraduates from the very beginning both points them in that direction and qualifies them to take part.

11.
Some Principal Concerns in the Shaping of Sociology

JOHN SCOTT

This has been an interesting and useful conference. As immediate past-President of the British Sociological Association, I would like to thank Chelly Halsey for organizing the intellectual programme of the conference and to thank the British Academy for the financial and administrative support it has provided.

It will be impossible in the space available to summarize the many diverse papers and the stimulating issues that they have raised. Those papers can, in any case, stand for themselves in this publication. What I would like to do, however, is to highlight some of the central themes that, in my mind, have recurred through the course of the various papers and discussions and seem to be the principal areas of concern.

I will focus on the issues of disciplinarity, globalization, source material, and the quantitative–qualitative division.

Disciplinarity

We have heard a number of views that make it clear that it is important to distinguish between the intellectual differentiation of scientific activities and the disciplinary divisions through which they are pursued.

Disciplines are competing and autonomous groupings of researchers and teachers that are, in crucial respects, historically arbitrary. They each arise at particular points in history, in a context of already established disciplines, and are best understood as pragmatic responses to practical—and often political—issues. They are concretely institutionalized social entities with

136

characteristics that change over time in response to internal and external demands. Any particular pattern of disciplines involves a division of scientific labour that is, in crucial respects, a negotiated outcome of a particular balance of power among socially organized academics. We have heard about the formation of university-based sociology from the concerns of 'amateurs' and those affiliated to other disciplines, and we have heard about the key role played by professional associations in shaping this.

The differentiation of disciplines, therefore, will rarely map onto any scheme of intellectual differentiation. Attempts to differentiate disciplines by their concern with particular and exclusive intellectual problems are doomed to failure. Real life is messier than our intellectual schemes. It has and will always be the case that there will be areas of common concern that unite adherents of different disciplines and, equally, areas of disagreement that divide them. For this reason, it is difficult to characterize sociology as concerned with one set of intellectual issues and to give it exclusive jurisdiction over these. Historians, geographers, and others will challenge such claims and may even regard some or all of those issues as coming within their remit.

Nevertheless, I do think that there is a sense in which sociology can be distinguished from other social sciences. There is a general framework of ideas about social relations that may be the *common* concern of the social sciences but is the *particular* concern of sociology. This centres on the idea of what it is to talk about human 'society' in all its complexity. The discipline of sociology is the specific promoter and guardian of these concerns, though they run through the various social sciences and many other social sciences have made crucial contributions to their development. Without the institutionalization of sociology as a discipline, such a framework of general ideas could never have been established and sustained by the separate and more specialized disciplines.

There is a sense in which this claim makes me look like a sociological imperialist, but I am not trying to claim that sociology alone develops these ideas and then makes them available for 'application' by under-labouring specialists in subordinate disciplines. Those in other disciplines do, of course, draw on ideas developed by sociologists—though not, perhaps, as often as sociologists would like to believe. Equally important, however, is the fact that other social scientists themselves produce ideas that can be regarded as sociological and as making a contribution to the general framework of ideas that I have alluded to. When considering the intellectual value of particular ideas, the disciplinary affiliation of their producers is rarely important.

Thus, the fact, as we have been told, that social historians have made less use of sociological work than might be expected (at least by sociologists) does not mean that work in social history is not sociological. It is not too unrealistic to hold that, despite his trenchant criticisms of sociology, Edward Thompson was a very good sociologist whose work on class has had a major impact on those working within the discipline of sociology. Card-carrying sociologists have no monopoly over the production of sociological ideas.

All this points to the fluidity of disciplinary boundaries, and there are, I think, two main implications that must be recognized. First, there is the permeability of disciplinary boundaries; second, there is the restructuring of disciplines.

The permeability of disciplinary boundaries was especially apparent in the nineteenth century and early twentieth century before the university departmental system was firmly crystallized. Those who produced sociological ideas and engaged in debate with each other were not merely 'sociologists'. Indeed, this is neatly encapsulated in Martin Bulmer's question of 'who counts as a sociologist?' John Peel usefully emphasizes the sibling relationship of sociology and social anthropology—though, like all siblings, they may sometimes fall out and come to regard one another as mortal enemies. Similar points can be made about the fruitful debates and dialogues among those who may, today, be claimed by geography, psychology, economics, political science, or history.

I recall sitting on a selection panel when an economic historian present had the temerity to speak approvingly of Max Weber's work in economic history. 'Oh no,' said the Vice-Chancellor—also a sociologist—'he's one of ours!' Pioneering figures come to be recognized as totemic figures for disciplines—legitimating their claims with respect to others—even where the pioneer him or herself may have made very different disciplinary claims.

In fact, sociological discourse in its formative period—the period of so-called 'classical sociology'—was highly diverse and was the product of those affiliated to many disciplines and none. A striking feature of the crystallization and autonomization of disciplines has been a reduction in the degree of intellectual exchange between different disciplines: a trend that many would regard as undesirable in itself and as dangerous for sociology. While disciplinary permeability has obvious dangers—not least a possible loss of intellectual identity for the participants—it has equally obvious benefits for all concerned.

The restructuring of disciplines has particular salience for sociology. This restructuring has largely come about through the growing internal specialization of the subject. In his contribution to the conference Martin Trow pointed out that specialization within sociology has been a marked feature of the growth of the discipline, as it has of other social sciences. Those specializing in such areas as the sociology of medicine and the sociology of crime, for example, have taken their specialisms as increasingly important areas of intellectual identification. This specialization has been associated with a growth of interdisciplinary work: specialists in medical sociology are likely to have as many, if not more, intellectual contacts with epidemiologists and socially oriented specialists in medicine and biology as they are with other sociologists. In many cases, interdisciplinary work leads to the formation of new disciplines that split off from their former 'parents'.

An implication of this concurrent specialization and interdisciplinary focus is what, in his contribution to the conference, John Goldthorpe referred to as the 'disorganization' of the discipline of sociology. Parts of sociology have, indeed, declined or disappeared as interdisciplinary areas have been departmentalized as new or revamped disciplines. The growth of management and business schools has gone hand in hand with the demise of many parts of industrial sociology and the sociology of organizations. The growth of political science and government has been associated with the demise of political sociology. The growth of health studies and criminology (and, at one time, of social policy) has also been at the expense of areas of sociology and may continue to be so in the future. Sociology is in danger, as John Urry once pointed out, of becoming a residual discipline, consisting of those working on whatever is left over after others have had their choice of the prime real estate.

The growth of cultural and media studies perhaps points to other dangers. These disciplines are far closer to what is 'left over' after the politics, economics, crime, and health have been taken out. If we lose these too, what is sociology to be left with? Go into any branch of Waterstone's and look for the sociology books: they are already filed under 'Cultural Studies', just next to 'Mind, Body, and Spirit'.

While it may be gratifying that many other disciplines have become sociologized, the danger is that core areas of sociology disappear and we are left with a ragbag of residual odds and ends. The solution must be, as both Jennifer Platt and Colin Crouch suggest, to ensure that core concerns are adequately represented in our teaching syllabuses. We must ensure that the design of degree courses reflects general intellectual concerns rather than market pressures and specialized research interests. Those general ideas about social relations that I earlier alluded to and the ways in which they have been explored by 'sociologists' must figure centrally in the training of future generations of sociologists. The concept of 'society' must be brought back in to become the unifying centre of the discipline: sociology needs to once again define itself as the 'study of society'.

Globalization

We have been concentrating our attention on British sociology, though with some international comparisons and commentaries. However, we have not really addressed the question of whether there is any such thing as a distinctly 'British' sociology. There is certainly sociology that happens to have been undertaken in Britain, but this is not the same thing. We have to ask if there is anything distinctively British about British sociology.

Dominique Schnapper has referred to the parochialism of sociology today. In all countries, the perhaps surprising feature of academic work is the relative lack of interest in studies undertaken in other countries. This is not a universal reaction, but it is certainly very common.

The situation can, perhaps, be contrasted with the situation as it was in the formative period of the late nineteenth century. Chelly Halsey and others have shown how *international* 'British sociology' was, from its very earliest days. Indeed, the whole development of sociology in the formative period can be characterized as a global phenomenon. It might be suggested that this is a reflection of social marginality: the marginal intellectuals in each country, marginalized because of their engagement in the pursuit of sociology,

140

sought mutual support from each other and built up transnational networks to supplement their relatively weak national networking with those engaged in longer established disciplines in the arts and sciences.

We need consider only the global impact of Auguste Comte and Herbert Spencer. Spencer was published and translated in many countries, from the USA to Japan, while Comte received, if anything, even greater coverage. Harriet Martineau's condensed English translation of Comte's *Cours* proved so successful that it was even translated back into French. But, who now reads Benjamin Kidd, whose books sold in massive numbers world-wide (including both the USA and China), exceeding even the sales achieved by Spencer? Le Play, rarely read today, was one of the most widely read empirical sociologists. The *Sociological Papers* show clearly the international character of correspondents and contributors to debates.

The identification of 'national' sociologies may be a useful and convenient basis for analysis and comparison, allowing us to see what is generic and what is specific, but we must not assume that it is the most appropriate or meaningful unit of intellectual activity. A national focus may be equally as arbitrary as a disciplinary focus, reflecting funding regimes, career structures, and political matters rather than purely intellectual concerns. National disciplines, as I have suggested, may be flags of convenience for funding and career purposes, but may not be the units by which intellectual advance (or regression) can be measured. It is, at the very least, important to problematize national disciplinary boundaries and to recognize that they may change over time.

There has always been a high level of interchange between British and other sociologists. Although it is difficult to assess or to quantify, my impression is that there were more translations of foreign works of general sociology into English, relative to the total number of publications, than there are today. It is certainly the case that there was a regular interchange of academic visitors at conferences and workshops and that scholars from various countries knew each other well. As an example, the copy of a book by the French functionalist René Worms held at the library of the London School of Economics (and perhaps once owned by Hobhouse) is inscribed, in French, 'To my dear friend and colleague, Ferdinand Tönnies'.

A particularly striking trend, I believe, has been that the increasing specialization of intellectual activity has been associated with the establishment of transnational links between specialisms. Instead of different specialist areas being closely integrated with each other as parts of a 'national' sociology, they are today more likely to be linked with other similar specialisms in other countries. Transnational specialities may be becoming more important and more salient foci of solidarity than national disciplines. Transnational 'organic' solidarity may be replacing 'mechanical' national solidarities.

Source Material

We have heard about research based on the use of a number of different sources, all of which have proved fruitful in research into the history of British sociology. These have included books and other published works, questionnaire surveys, interviews, and archives of documents. We should not forget, however, that information technology is transforming the ways in which archives are built and maintained. Much of the potential source material for historical research in the future, including the minutes of professional associations and teaching departments, reading lists, and study materials, will be electronic. Much of this already appears as web pages.

Little or nothing is systematically archived from these electronic sources. How many of us routinely keep copies of our old word-processing files once they are no longer of current 'relevance' for research or teaching activities? We have been reminded by Jennifer Platt of the insecurity and non-survival of departmental and professional files stored in broom cupboards, but how many electronic files even get into the cupboard in the first place? Even where back-up takes place, the resulting electronic archives are, typically, progressively deleted as new material is archived. We have looked at the problems inherent in relying on memories held in the minds of individuals, but what attention are we giving to the absence of an electronic archive? The British Library is beginning to archive some electronic materials, but the kinds of sources that will be of interest to future historians of sociology may not be covered. (Though see the Wayback Machine at www.archive.org/web/web.php.)

Quality and Quantity in Research Methods

A persistent undercurrent in the discussions has been the suggestion that British sociology has come to be overly concerned with qualitative research and shows a corresponding lack of skills in quantitative methods. The suggestion, perhaps, is that sociology originated as the 'science of society', but finds it difficult to lay claim to expertise on either of these nouns. The most critical of the speakers has been Robert Erikson, whose remarks led John Goldthorpe to suggest that a growing lack of quantitative skills might presage a complete fragmentation of the discipline.

The quantitative skills of the sociologists of the formative period should not be overstated—most were very weak in this respect—but it can, perhaps, be agreed that there are relatively fewer works containing numbers than was the case in the 1950s and 1960s. Articles using quantitative methods are now rare in the leading journals in Britain, and this trend is more marked than in many other countries.

It is important, however, to see a difference between recognizing a lack of quantitative research and quantitative skills, on the one hand, and denying the need for qualitative research. We have to be concerned not with the type of research, but with its quality. As Colin Crouch has pointed out, the key question is not a division between 'quantitative' and 'qualitative' work, but the contrast between the appropriate or inappropriate handling of evidence and argument. Qualitative case studies and qualitative investigations with small numbers of cases are perfectly acceptable forms of research, so long as the handling of evidence and the drawing of conclusions are systematic, critical, and disciplined.

The key question, surely, is the appropriate balance between the quantitative and qualitative, and the way to alter this balance is to increase the amount of good quantitative work, not to reduce the amount of good qualitative work. To put it that way, of course, is to state the problem rather than to suggest any solutions. To work towards a solution, the British Sociological Association has begun working with the Learning and Teaching

Support Network (www.c-sap.bham.ac.uk/projects/findings/ ShowFinding.asp?id=34) to collate and disseminate information on best practice in the training of undergraduate sociologists.

I hope that those who attended the conference and read its presentations will not be too pessimistic over the talk of the disintegration of the discipline and the possible loss of the archives of the future. We have heard as many positive points. As Jennifer Platt noted, this year is the fiftieth anniversary of a number of sociological organizations, and we have been hearing a lot about the real achievements made during those years. I hope that at least some of those attending the conference might be able to come back in fifty years time to see who got it right.